A Wild Australia Guide

SPIDERS

PATRICK HONAN

Above: The Peacock Jumping Spider is one of Australia's more colourful species.
Cover: Green Tree Ant-mimicking Spider.

Contents

Introduction

Spiders have long been one of the most successful groups of animals on earth. Since they first appeared nearly 360 million years ago, they have been major contributors to land-based ecosystems and today they play a vital role in the unique and complex wildlife systems that make up the Australian environment.

A COLOURFUL ARRAY

Although generally considered drab, repulsive and hairy, spiders display a remarkable array of body shapes and colours. Some are delicately fragile — others range in shape from spherical to triangular, hexagonal or square. They are often beautifully patterned with reds, blues, greens and yellows, or adorned with silver, gold and iridescent colours that vary with changing light.

There are 35,000 known species of spiders worldwide and more than 2000 of these live in Australia. It is estimated that this is only one quarter of the number that actually exist. Australian spiders range in size from the 55 mm-long whistling (or bird-eating) spiders (*Selenocosmia* sp.) to litter-dwelling species that measure less than a millimetre in length.

WHERE DO THEY FIT IN?

Spiders belong to a class of arthropods called "arachnids", named after the maiden Arachne from Greek Mythology. The fable tells, she was a skilled weaver who was changed into a spider as punishment for her pride. The class Arachnida also includes scorpions, pseudoscorpions, harvestmen, mites and ticks, but only spiders belong to the order Araneae within this class. Spiders are often confused with insects, which are unrelated and belong to the class Insecta.

Top: Jumping spiders are often brightly coloured but many species are adorned with more subtle stripes and patterns. **Left:** Certain spiders use both camouflage and mimicry to avoid predators and deceive prey. This crab spider imitates Green Tree Ants.

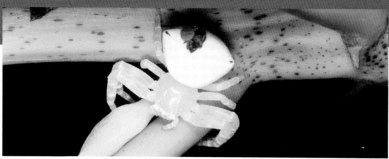

THE FIRST SPIDERS

The first spiders were probably remarkably similar to many which survive today. They were large, drab, ground-dwelling creatures, probably living in shallow tunnels lined with silk. While these early spiders did produce silk, it was not used to its full benefit until millions of years later when web-making techniques evolved. The most ancient group of living spiders (called Hypochilomorphs) still survive today in eastern Australia and Tasmania, part of our remarkable spider fauna.

This fauna includes many species that are found nowhere else. Spiders range from deserts to caves, streams to seashores and alpine country to rainforests. Most of the species that live here are restricted to Australia but some are also found overseas and several species have been introduced from Australia to other countries.

Top: The tiny brown male can be seen on the back of this much larger female White Crab Spider (*Thomisus spectabilis*). **Right, top to bottom:** Orb-weaving spiders come in an amazing array of shapes and patterns; Spiders are often able to capture prey many times their own size; Huntsmans are very well known in Australia; Spiders capture millions upon millions of insects around the world.

Body Parts

Spiders are characterised by having two body parts, joined by a narrow waist. The first part is a fusion of the head and middle section (together called the "cephalothorax"), which bears the eyes, mouthparts and legs and is covered with a shield-like carapace. The second part is the abdomen, containing reproductive and digestive organs, silk glands and the "spinnerets".

THE FRONT HALF

At the front of a spider's head are its fangs — hollow, needle-like structures used to capture and kill prey, and for defence. Behind the fangs are a pair of appendages called the pedipalps, which basically act as touch receptors. Mature males bear enlarged sex organs at the end of their pedipalps, which they wave at females during courtship displays. These organs are the major external difference between males and females, but females are also generally larger than males.

Top: Spider bodies have two parts, with the front bearing the legs and the back the internal organs.
Above, left to right: The eyes of wolf spiders are specially adapted to see at night. They have large mirrors within, which may give off a green glow; Spiders' fangs are attached to two stout "chelicerae" at the front of the head. They can be flexed in and out at will; The male Net-casting Spider's pedipalps bear enlarged organs used to transfer sperm to the female during mating. **Opposite, below:** The long spinnerets are visible at the tip of the abdomen of this whistling (or bird-eating) spider.

cephalothorax — — — — —
pedipalps — — — — — — — — — — — — — — spinnerets
fangs — — — —
chelicerae — — — —
eyes — — — — — — — — — — — — — — abdomen
— — — — — — — — leg

FEATURES OF A SPIDER

GETTING AROUND

Spiders have four pairs of walking legs, variable in form and function but generally simple and unspecialised. In most spiders the two front pairs of legs point forwards and the two back pairs face backwards. In groups such as huntsman and crab spiders, the legs are turned sideways so that the "knees" point towards the back of the body, enabling the spider to walk in very confined places such as under bark. The legs usually end in a pair of claws which may be surrounded by tufts of fine hairs that help the spider walk up vertical surfaces and upside down on ceilings. Each tuft may contain 1000 tiny individual hairs. These tufts also help some spiders walk across water.

THE BACK HALF

The main external feature of the abdomen is the spinnerets — segmented finger-like appendages from which the silk is drawn. Most spiders have three pairs of spinnerets. At least six groups of Australian spiders (including humped spiders (*Uloborus* spp.), net-casting spiders (*Deinopis* and *Avella* spp.) and house spiders (*Badumna* spp.) also have a special spinning plate called the "cribellum", just in front of the spinnerets, which is used to comb out wide ribbons of silk.

Senses

Spiders are as well tuned to their environment as any other group of animals and are probably aware of their surroundings in ways we don't yet understand.

A SENSE OF MOVEMENT

The simplest sense is the detection of vibrations. Spiders living on foliage are able to pick up mechanical vibrations along a leaf signalling the approach of a predator, prey or potential mate. The bodies of most spiders are covered in special hairs and slit-like organs in the exoskeleton designed to detect the tiniest of air movements, again signalling the presence of danger or food. During courtship, a male orb-weaver will sit at the edge of a female's web and pluck the outer strands, signalling his approach onto the web.

SINGING SPIDERS

Some spiders are able to produce sound as well as detect it. Whistling (or bird-eating) spiders (*Selenocosmia* spp.) make a rasping sound by rubbing their fangs against a file-like structure just to one side of the chelicerae. This is done as a warning when the spider is disturbed. A range of other spiders, particularly overseas species, have been shown to make and detect sound.

TASTY FEET

Many spiders also have a well developed sense of smell and taste. Perhaps the most important role for their sense of smell is to pick up pheromones produced by members of the opposite sex. This is essential as most species are nocturnal and have poor eyesight. Taste is detected by specialised hairs on the tips of the legs and pedipalps, enabling the spider to determine whether a potential prey item is toxic or edible.

Top, left: Many spiders, such as whistling spiders, have very small eyes and rely heavily on other senses. **Above:** The leg-like pedipalps at the front of the body are not used for walking, but are scent, taste and touch receptors.

THE EYES HAVE IT

Most spiders have eight eyes, each consisting of just one lens, that can detect no more than light or dark, or just movement alone. However, jumping spiders and net-casting spiders have an extremely well-developed pair of front eyes. Jumping Spiders have 360° vision and can see moving objects up to 40 cm away. They hunt by sight during the day and will leap across considerable gaps onto unsuspecting prey. Certain types of spider appear to be able to detect ultraviolet light and polarised light, both of which are invisible to humans.

Top, right: Spiders' bodies are covered with sensory hairs of different lengths. The hairs can be seen on the legs of this female as she guards her young on their egg sac. **Above:** Aside from their large eyes, wolf spiders (*Lycosa* spp.) pick up vibrations from the ground to alert them to the presence of both predators and prey.

Of all the billions of spiders that are born every day on Earth, more than 99% of them die before reaching adulthood. They are preyed upon by other spiders, a range of insects, scorpions, centipedes, fish, frogs, reptiles, birds and mammals. They also suffer from diseases and are attacked by fungi and parasitic worms.

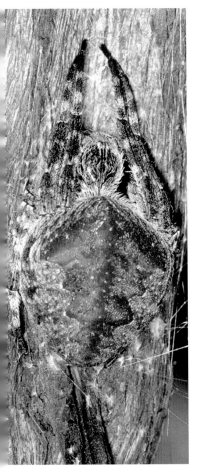

Above: During the day, Garden Orb-weavers (*Eriophora biapicata*) curl up their bodies on a branch or trunk and are easily overlooked by predators.

THE WORM TURNS

One of the most bizarre groups of creatures to attack spiders are Gordian Worms. These worms are long and thin and live in freshwater, where they lay thousands of eggs. The newly hatched worms may be eaten by freshwater insect larvae which eventually mature with the dormant worms inside and leave the water. The insect is then eaten by a spider, after which the worm breaks its dormancy, burrows out through the spider's stomach and feeds on its internal organs. When the spider eventually dies, the worm emerges from the dead body and makes its way back to the water.

FLY EATS SPIDER

Many types of parasitic insects, particularly flies and wasps, also attack spiders. These parasites, technically called "parasitoids" because they eventually kill their hosts, may attack the eggs, spiderlings or adult spiders. An Ichneumon Wasp, for example, will lay an egg on the outside of a spider and, when the egg hatches, the tiny larva burrows into the skin and feeds on its host's internal organs. The spider continues to feed and behave naturally, until the burden of the parasite overwhelms it. Spider-Hunting Wasps use the same strategy but instead of leaving the spider in place, the wasp paralyses the host and carries it back to the nest. An egg is laid on the spider and it is sealed up either in a burrow or in a nest made from dried mud.

THE BEST DEFENCE

A spider's most effective strategy in defence of all attacks is to hide. Most spiders are active nocturnally, avoiding birds and most of the parasitic wasps and flies. During the day they hide under bark or underground, or camouflage themselves so superbly they are almost impossible to see.

Top: Turret Spiders (*Dolophones turrigera*) not only wrap themselves around a branch during the day, but their abdomen is topped with a "turret"which looks like a broken off twig. **Centre, left to right:** Two-tailed Spiders are so perfectly camouflaged on tree trunks they are almost impossible to see; Same photograph with spider outlined. **Above, left to right:** This Leaf Rolling Crab Spider has been parasitised by tiny wasps. A hatched white egg can be seen on its cephalothorax; Mud Wasps collect living spiders and entomb them in nests made from dried mud; Ground-dwelling spiders, like this Wolf Spider are often striped or mottled, allowing them to blend in with leaf litter.

Silk

Spider silk is best known for its role in web construction, but it has many other uses. It is used to construct trip lines by burrowing spiders, as a net by net-casting spiders, as a safety line to anchor huntsman spiders as they hunt and to wrap dangerous prey once caught. It is also used to line burrows, build shelters and protect the spider during the delicate process of moulting. Female spiders may use silk to build a safe shelter for laying eggs and some species wrap the eggs in silken egg sacs for further protection. Male spiders use silk to transfer sperm to females during mating and the males of some species use it to tie the female down during courtship.

STRONGER THAN STEEL

Spider silk is the strongest known natural fibre — five times stronger than steel and yet much more flexible. Depending on the type of silk, it can be stretched to more than twice its own length, and is excellent at absorbing energy, enabling the spider to sit safely in the centre of its web. Silk is often clear but it can come in a range of colours, including green, blue, brown and black. Some spiders produce silver or golden silk, which catches the sunlight to give a magnificent display.

LIQUID SILK

Silk is about 50% protein and is produced as a liquid within silk glands. Strands of silk are extruded from spinnerets at the tip of the abdomen and drawn out by the spider with its back legs. The strength of the silk may be determined by how quickly it is extruded. There are seven different types of silk known. All spiders produce at least three different types of silk but no spider possesses all seven possible types. Garden Orb-weavers (*Eriophora transmarina*) and Golden Orb-weavers (*Nephila* spp.) each have five different types.

Spiders usually have three pairs of spinnerets and their size and arrangement varies between different spider families. In most spiders, the spinnerets can be seen just protruding from the tip of the abdomen, but groups such as Two-tailed Spiders (*Tamopsis* spp.) may have exceptionally long spinnerets.

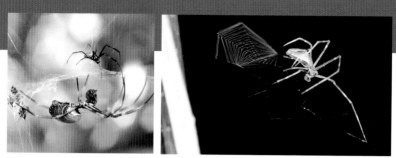

Clockwise from top left: Spiders produce silk in different colours, sometimes in different circumstances. One of the most common colours is gold; Net-casting spiders construct support strands from one type of silk and nets from another; The tough silk of the egg sac (in this case that of the White-tailed Spider, *Lampona* sp.) is sometimes broken open by predators to get at the eggs within; Spiders like this huntsman do not build webs for catching prey, but lay down a silken safety line wherever they travel. **Opposite, top:** Most spiders wrap their eggs in tough protective silk. This silk differs from other types used to build webs.

Web Building

Perhaps the most well-known feature of spiders is their ability to build webs. This has been developed into an art form by the orb-weavers. Webs are not always built vertically but also horizontally and every angle in between, sometimes in several layers covered with a protective tent-like roof of silk.

A WORLD OF WEBS

Some comb-footed spiders, like the Grey House Spider (*Achaearanea tepidariorum*), construct "tangle webs" in corners, made up of a mass of strands reaching to the ground. While they appear random, there is method to these webs — the strong dry threads enable the spider to move in any direction. "Sheet webs", made by species such as the Comb-footed Platform Spider (*Achaearanea mundula*), comprise a thick, messy sheet of silk draped amongst foliage or in tree hollows. A number of spiders build a type of orb web which is not a complete circle and is supported by a mass of untidy strands.

THE WEB MASTERS

Construction of an orb web is a long and precise process. To begin, the spider sits in a prominent position and plays out silk from the spinnerets, to be carried away by the slightest breeze until the end attaches to a solid object. The spider then pulls the strand tight and drops downwards, often to the ground, to attach the framework at the base. When the frame is in place, the spider constructs between twenty and 60 spokes, radiating out from the centre, around which the sticky spiral is spun. The spiral is the catching area of the web and takes the longest to build. As each thread is attached, the spider uses its hindleg to pull the thread taut, breaking up the sticky coating into tiny globules like beads on a necklace.

An orb-weaving spider may produce more than 20 m of silk to build a web. The hub of a web, where the spider usually sits, is built closer to the top than the bottom. Because it takes the spider longer to run uphill than down once prey has been trapped.

Left: There are many different species commonly referred to as Golden Orb-weaver (*Nephila edulis*, pictured), only the scientific name changes.

Clockwise from top left: Spiders such as the St Andrew's Cross Spider (*Argiope keyserlingi*) decorate their webs with special silk that reflects ultraviolet light; Some species sit in the web at night but desert it during the day. Others, like this species of Golden Orb-weaver (*Nephilia maculata*), remain in the web both day and night; Orb webs are held in place by a framework attached to solid objects. The framework may be left in place while the web is removed and rebuilt.

Shelters

Most spider species build some sort of shelter in which to hide from the elements and predators. These are usually made from silk and may incorporate leaves or bark to enhance their camouflage. Some spiders, such as clubionid spiders, retain the same shelter throughout life, while others construct temporary shelters for particular purposes. As they grow, many spiders will construct a moulting chamber and abandon it as soon as the new skin hardens. Most females produce egg sacs in a specially constructed brood chamber. Jumping spiders and crab spiders will often use a single leaf, rolled and sewn together with silk, to moult and lay eggs in. Huntsman spiders shelter under bark and the female, when ready to produce eggs, will seal all the cracks in the bark with thick sheets of silk.

A PLACE OF THEIR OWN

Many web spinners attach a shelter to the edge of their web. House spiders and comb-footed spiders construct a funnel-like retreat at the back or top of their web, into which they flee when threatened. Feeding, moulting, mating and egg-laying may also take place within the same retreat. Perhaps the best known retreat is that of the Leaf-curling Spider (*Phonognatha graeffei*), which lifts a single leaf from the ground, twists it into shape and shelters within.

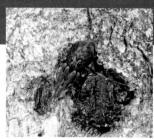

A LIFE UNDERGROUND

Wolf spiders, trapdoor spiders and whistling (or bird-eating) spiders dig sometimes elaborate burrows underground, particularly in arid areas. Some species plug the burrow with a trapdoor made from soil and silk, while others build tall chimneys or turrets around the entrance to stop the burrow flooding during heavy rain.

Because they are vulnerable to invading predators such as centipedes, many burrowing species have developed interesting techniques to escape. Some burrows have two entrances and others have a false bottom under which the resident spider can hide without being detected. Mouse Spider (*Missulena bradleyi*) and trapdoor spider burrows may have a short tunnel off to the side of the main shaft, hidden by a flimsy door, into which the spider can retreat when invaded.

Clockwise from top left: Spiders such as the Black House Spider (*Badumna insignis*) will do without a shelter at times when they are able to camouflage themselves on a suitable background; A large female huntsman sheltering in a small cavity in the bark. She will use the same shelter to lay eggs; Desert species such as this whistling (or bird-eating) spider dig burrows to escape the heat of the sun. **Opposite, top:** Sheet webs built over the ground provide shelter for some spiders and collect dew in the early mornings. **Opposite, bottom:** The silken shelter of a female Northern Green Jumping Spider (*Mopsus mormon*) is constructed to protect the spider and her eggs.

Colours

The right colour and pattern is essential to the survival of a spider, allowing it to both capture prey and avoid predators. Colour is produced by pigments underneath the spider's hard outer "cuticle" (skin) and their brightness is in part determined by the presence of a substance called "sclerotin", which is used to strengthen the cuticle. Areas where strength is required and sclerotin is abundant, such as the chelicerae, tend to be dark. Areas requiring more flexibility, such as the joints, tend to be paler. In addition to these pigments, many groups, such as jumping spiders, sport brilliantly iridescent colours using microscopic structures on the body or hairs which refract light. In this way they can produce any colour imaginable, including metallic golds and silvers.

QUICK COLOUR CHANGE

The St Andrew's Cross Spider (*Argiope keyserlingi*) can change the brightness of its yellow bands by expanding or contracting its abdomen. The changing shape alters the angle of light striking the covering of hairs, making the colour more vibrant when threatened.

The Two-spined Spider (*Poecilopachys australasia*) pumps special fluid through the outer layer of the cuticle when disturbed, producing rapid waves of subtle colour changes through the yellow and around the outer edges. Some species of crab spiders, as well as the Garden Orb-weaver (*Eriophora biapicata*), are able to change their overall colour slightly to blend in with their environment.

Top: Some spiders, such as this Spiny Spider (*Gasteracantha sacerdtalis*), are more colourful than butterflies. **Left:** Many spiders are boldly patterned with contrasting colours and intricately detailed lines.

COLOUR FOR SURVIVAL

Most spiders, particularly ground-dwelling species, are a drab brown or grey to blend in with their environment. Spiders living on tree trunks tend to be mottled brown to match their habitat. Those spiders that are active in broad daylight and do not blend in with their background may adopt a different strategy. A combination of red and black is generally used as a warning to advertise that the owner is dangerous, as with the Red-back Spider (*Latrodectus hasselti*). Red and Black Spiders (*Ambicodamus crinitus*) roam tree trunks during the day but appear to be protected by their bright red and black markings. These spiders are not known to be poisonous, so the strategy is probably an effective bluff.

Top, right: The White Crab Spider (*Thomisus spetabilis*) is one of the few completely white spiders, with a beautifully translucent cephalothorax. **Above, left to right:** Jumping spiders like this Northern Green Jumping Spider (*Mopsus mormon*) are active during the day and are often brightly coloured; Spiders that live in foliage are often green, sometimes with stripes of yellow or white to break up their outlines; The Red-back Spider advertises that it is dangerous with a bright red warning stripe.

Mating & Egg Laying

Mating can be a risky business, particularly for male spiders — the male is often many times smaller than the female and, if she is not receptive to him, will become another meal for her. Males of many species cease feeding and web-building as soon as they mature, spending their time searching for females. In order to properly identify himself as a potential mate, the male may undertake an elaborate courtship dance, with the female's response determining whether he will approach close enough to mate. Courtship may begin with the male offering the female a dead insect.

A RISKY DANCE

Male Long-jawed Spiders have specially adapted chelicerae designed to hold the fangs of the female apart to prevent her eating him. Male funnelwebs have spurs on their front legs for the same purpose and some male crab spiders tie the female down with silk from which she breaks free soon after the male departs.

GETTING IN CLOSE

Sperm transfer in spiders is unusually complicated. Before mating, the male produces sperm from an opening underneath his abdomen and deposits it on a small sheet of silk called a "sperm web". The sperm is then sucked up by the male's pedipalps ready to be transferred into the female's reproductive opening. Consequently, mating takes place with both sexes holding onto each other, close enough for the male to reach under her body and into the opening with one or both of his pedipalps. In some species, the male breaks off the tip of the pedipalp once it is in place to make sure it remains there securely.

Left: The size difference between male and female spiders is often enormous, as with this pair of St Andrew's Cross Spiders. **Opposite, clockwise from top right:** Female wolf spiders carry their eggs around with them; This female spider is sharing a queen sugar ant with her young; The egg sac of the Six-spined Spider is wrapped around a twig and abandoned by the female; Emerging huntsman spiderlings often require their mother to open the tough silk of the egg sac; Many spiders, like this Long-jawed Spider, care for their young after they hatch.

THE NEXT GENERATION

All spiders reproduce by laying eggs, which come in a vast array of sizes and colours — green, white and pink being the most common. The eggs are usually deposited in an egg sac made of tough silk which may be guarded by the female until they hatch. Most orb-weaving spiders hide the egg sac in foliage at the edge of the web. The female Daddy Long-legs wraps the egg mass in a few strands of silk and carries it in her chelicerae.

Growth & Development

Spider eggs have large yolks compared with those of insects and, in any batch of eggs, there are often infertile eggs left by the mother to provide the spiderlings' first meal. Because their exoskeleton does not stretch, spiders shed their skin as they grow; the first of these moults often takes place within the egg sac.

DOTING MOTHERS

The females of some huntsman and crab spiders must cut a hole in the egg sac in order for the spiderlings to emerge, otherwise they starve to death. In a number of spider groups, the female cares for the young before they disperse. She may catch prey and share it with them or, in the case of some comb-footed spiders, actively feed them from her mouth. In many species, the female dies soon after the spiderlings hatch and she becomes their first meal.

Wolf spiders (*Lycosa* spp.) are perhaps the most devoted mothers — the female carries the egg sac with her everywhere, attached to the end of her abdomen. When the eggs hatch, the spiderlings climb onto her back and hold on to specially designed knob-shaped hairs on her abdomen until they are old enough to disperse.

A TOUGH LIFE

After hatching, spiderlings of most species play out a long line of silk on which they "balloon" away to disperse on the slightest breeze. This is remarkably effective, as spiderlings have been found more than 4 km above the Earth. Once they land, the young spiders begin to feed almost immediately and web-spinning species set up their first web, usually slightly different in form to webs spun later in life.

Predators are a constant threat from the moment the eggs are laid and small parasitic wasps and flies which lay their own eggs on the spiders account for a large mortality rate. Moulting is a particularly dangerous time, when the spider's body is soft and immobile for an extended period and is vulnerable to even the smallest predators. As a consequence of all these trials, usually less than one percent of spiders survive to maturity and these are indeed lucky spiders.

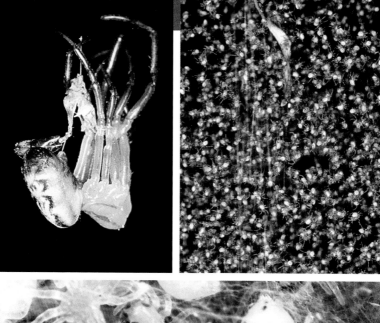

Clockwise from top left: A Leaf-curling Spider (*Phonognatha* sp.) moulting. The spider is hanging upside down with its legs still to be drawn out from the old skin; A single egg sac from a female spider may produce hundreds of spiderlings, but only a tiny fraction will survive to adulthood; These newly hatched Northern Green Jumping Spiders (*Mopsus mormon*) are very similar to the adults in both shape and colour. **Opposite:** Baby wolf spiders cling to the back of their mother's abdomen for some time after being born.

Spiders & Their Prey

Spiders feed largely on living insects and have developed a range of remarkable adaptations to capture and consume them. They are, however, generalist predators and will consume any prey of suitable size, including most invertebrates and some small fish, reptiles, birds and even mammals. Spiders frequently eat other spiders and even members of their own species. They will feed on eggs, spiderlings, potential mating partners and some species even consume their own mothers. In comparison to their own size, spiders have the largest range of prey size in the animal kingdom. A Golden Orb-weaver (*Nephila ornata*) feeds on anything trapped in its net, from the tiniest midges to small birds.

SURVIVAL INSTINCTS

The ability to take advantage of any opportunity is probably the result of surviving for millions of years with a general shortage of prey. Rarely do they live in an area of constant food supply. In order to cope with this situation, spiders have abdomens that are able to stretch enormously to accommodate a sudden increase in food and are able to store large amounts of fat. They have a very low metabolism and are able to continue to operate as predators on only one fifth of their normal energy requirements. When food is scarce, a spider will move its web or increase its territory to boost the chances of encountering prey. Young spiders may take longer to reach adulthood or even mature at a smaller size without sufficient food, but will reach maturity nonetheless.

PREYING TECHNIQUES

Spiders demonstrate some amazing adaptations for capturing prey. Bird-dropping Spiders (*Celaenia kinbergi*) use female moth pheromones to attract male moths within reach. Net-casting Spiders like the species *Deinopis subrufa* weave tiny nets that they cast over insects that come within their reach, while fishing spiders (*Dolomedes* spp.) dive underwater in search of aquatic prey. Some spiders (such as *Myrmarachne* spp.) are accomplished mimics of ants, allowing them to move undetected amongst their prey. Some spiders sit and wait for prey (called the ambushers or web-spinners), others actively hunt and run down their prey (the hunters).

Top: This jumping spider has captured a young huntsman. **Opposite, clockwise from top:** A Black House Spider feeds on a cockroach; Triangular spiders sit with front legs spread open, awaiting passing prey; Some spiders imitate their prey to get close enough to capture them; Leaf-curling Spiders hunt near the safety of their shelter; Orb-weavers capture large prey using the strength and flexibility of their webs.

Venomous Spiders

Of Australia's 2000 known spiders, only twelve are thought to cause a serious bite reaction in humans and only two have proven potentially fatal. The twelve species to watch include the Wolf Spider (*Lycosa* sp.), Black House Spider (*Badumna insignis*), Sac Spider (*Cheiracanthium mordax*), Recluse Spider (*Loxosceles rufescens*), Badge Spider (*Neosparassus diana*) and a couple of species of Trapdoor Spiders and Funnelwebs. The only two known to cause a fatal reaction in humans are the Red-back Spider (*Latrodectus hasselti*) and the Sydney Funnelweb (*Atrax robustus*).

A BITING DILEMMA

Surprisingly little is known about the venom of most Australian spiders, even those that are generally considered to cause a serious reaction. In many cases, people bitten by these species show no reaction whatsoever. On the other hand, bites have not been recorded from most Australian species so the effect of their venom is unknown.

Spider bite data is difficult to gather as many suspected spider bites are in fact caused by an insect, a small prick when gardening or even a rash. Even when a bite is genuine, in most cases the spider is not observed or seen only as it disappears unidentified. Sometimes, the spider is subsequently squashed flat and unidentifiable. Even if the spider is successfully collected unharmed, it is often misidentified if not taken to a qualified spider expert.

Top, left: The Sydney Funnelweb is only one of a number of funnelweb species in Australia. The venom of many of these species, however, is unknown. **Above:** The Badge Spider is part of the huntsman family but, unlike more common species, this one can inflict a painful bite.

TWO INNOCENT VILLAINS

Many of the myths about spider bites are stirred up by the media and the internet. The Daddy Long-legs (*Pholcus phalangoides*) and White-tailed Spider (*Lampona cylindrata*) are two good examples. The Daddy Long-legs is widely believed to be the most venomous spider in the world, with fangs too small to penetrate human skin. Studies have shown, however, that Daddy Long-legs venom is mild, causing only a small local reaction if any. Studies have also shown that the White-tailed Spider, long thought to cause massive skin ulcerations and gangrene-like symptoms, causes only local persistent pain and a small irritating red lesion.

Top: Contrary to popular belief, the bite of the White-tailed Spider does not appear to cause serious harm. **Above, left to right:** The Red-back Spider has caused a number of deaths in Australia, but none since an antivenom was developed; Although not particularly venomous, whistling (or bird-eating) spiders have fangs up to 1 cm long which can cause considerable pain; Daddy Long-legs are widely believed to be the most venomous spider in the world. They are included here only to emphasise that they are completely harmless.

Backyard Spiders

The average Australian suburban backyard is home to hundreds of spiders of many different species. Most are tiny and never seen by the homeowner. A few species are large and colourful, all playing an essential role in the health of the garden.

ROUND-THE-CLOCK SERVICE

Consider the plight of a female moth intent on laying eggs on a prized garden plant. As it flies through the backyard at night, the moth must avoid the many extensive orb webs stretched across established flight paths. As it nears the plant, it encounters the webs of smaller orb-weavers strung amongst the foliage. Upon landing at its chosen plant, the moth may encounter a waiting huntsman or Sac Spider (*Cheiracanthium mordax*) patrolling the leaves. If it does manage to lay eggs and escape, jumping spiders or Badge Spiders (*Neosparassus diana*) may discover the nest and suck every single egg dry before they hatch. Any caterpillars that survive to hatch must face a continuous onslaught of crab spiders, lynx spiders, clubionid spiders and cell spiders. These spiders provide a natural pest control service in every backyard, 24 hours a day.

Around country homesteads where crops are grown, spiders play an even more important role. They are the most numerous predators in the ecosystem and one of the few classes of predators that are always present. They can also have an indirect impact on insect pests; many insects seem to be able to detect the presence of a spider on a plant, causing the insect to abandon that source of food and sometimes starve to death as a result.

SUBURBAN MIRACLES

Despite the benefits provided by suburban spiders, they are often greeted with revulsion and horror when encountered by the homeowner. However, spending an hour in the evening watching an orb-weaver spin its web provides an insight into one of Nature's true miracles. The spider meticulously constructs a wonder of mechanical engineering, only to consume the entire structure the following morning and start again the next night. Australians dramatically undervalue these remarkable creatures and their wondrous activities, all occurring in their own backyards.

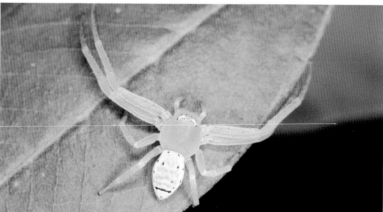

Above, top to bottom: Red-back Spiders frequent dark places in sheds, such as old plant pots. Most people are unaware of their presence; In gardens with plenty of flowering plants, crab spiders rest on the leaves and flowering heads awaiting prey; Small Brown Jumping Spiders (*Servea vestita*) are a common sight in backyards around Australia, usually seen foraging during the day. **Opposite, top:** The Garden Orb-weaver (*Eriophora biapicata*) is one of the most common and largest spiders in Australian backyards. **Opposite, bottom:** Miturgid spiders are common but rarely seen, they hide in silken shelters during the day and emerge at night.

Primitive Spiders
Order: Mygalomorphs

Spiders are classified in the Order Aranae, which is divided into two groups: the "primitive" spiders (Mygalomorphs) and the "advanced" spiders (Araneomorphs). The major distinction between the two groups is the way their fangs move. The fangs of primitive spiders strike downward like daggers, whereas those of advanced spiders move sidewards against each other like pincers. Most primitive spiders must therefore rear up before striking.

The primitive spider group includes funnelwebs, trapdoor spiders and whistling (or bird-eating) spiders. They are generally large, dark, hairy ground-dwelling spiders with a long life span. Whistling spiders are the largest spiders in Australia and belong to the tarantula family, which includes the largest spiders in the world. Most types spend almost all their time in burrows or under logs, but a couple of species live in holes in tree trunks. Different types of primitive spiders tend to look very similar to each other and have similar life styles.

Primitive spiders are still poorly studied in Australia. Until several years ago there were only two described species of whistling spiders in Australia and not many more species of funnelwebs. In reality Australia probably has at least a dozen species of whistling spiders and several dozen funnelweb species.

Top: When most people see a large black spider, they think of the Sydney Funnelweb, but there are a myriad of species living in all sorts of habitats.
Right: Trapdoor spiders are most commonly seen wandering around leaf litter at night.
Opposite: Although most primitive spiders are a uniform black or brown, some species have attractive markings on the abdomen or cephalothorax.

The females of this species are large, black, stoutly built spiders with impressively robust chelicerae. Their common name comes from their large size and burrowing habits. In contrast, the males are much smaller and coloured bright red in front and purple-blue behind.

DESCRIPTION: Females (pictured, below) are black all over whereas the cephalothorax of the male varies from bright red to orange-brown.

LIFE HISTORY: The female constructs an egg sac inside a brood chamber in the burrow. Her burrow is up to 30 cm deep and she sits at the entrance at night, awaiting passing prey. The brood chamber is at right angles to the main burrow, with a hinged door that is closed off to prevent predators entering. Unlike most primitive spiders, the spiderlings balloon away after hatching, probably accounting for their wide distribution. They feed on native snails, spiders and insects. Like other primitive spiders, mature males leave the burrow in search of females during winter and may be seen wandering in daylight.

BEHAVIOUR: These spiders spend most of their time in the burrow but will rear up and attempt to strike if cornered outside the burrow.

HABITAT: Found in a range of habitats across Australia, mostly along the banks of rivers and creeks.

VENOM: Laboratory trials suggest that the female can produce large quantities of toxic venom, but most people bitten have not suffered a serious reaction.

DISTRIBUTION: Occurs in all States except Tasmania.

SIZE: Male body length 15 mm, female 25 mm.

Southern Trapdoor Spider   *Stanwellia* sp.

This species is largely restricted to Melbourne and surrounds. In some areas it is abundant in every single backyard, although homeowners are usually completely unaware of its presence.

DESCRIPTION: Males are very similar to females (pictured, below) but sometimes have golden hairs on the front half of the body and always have longer legs.

LIFE HISTORY: Like most primitive spiders, this species is active at night. The female constructs an egg sac in her burrow, which is silk-lined and up to 40 cm deep. After hatching, the spiderlings leave and make their own burrows nearby, often resulting in large clusters of burrows over a small area. Despite this spider's name, its burrow does not have a trapdoor, but has several strands of silk radiating from the entrance, which the spider uses to detect passing prey as it sits at the top of the burrow at night. Mature males leave their burrows during autumn and wander in search of females,

often entering houses where they are sometimes mistaken for funnelwebs. Females may live more than five years.

BEHAVIOUR: This species is not aggressive but may bite if cornered. It remains in the burrow unless dug up accidentally by dogs or gardeners.

HABITAT: Found in dry forest, woodland and suburban areas.

VENOM: The bite is painful because of the size of the fangs, but the venom itself does not cause any serious problems.

DISTRIBUTION: Southern Victoria, particularly around Melbourne and its suburbs.

SIZE: Male body length 25 mm, female 35 mm.

Right: Southern Trapdoor Spiders are somewhat variable in colour and pattern, but generally black in front and brown behind.

These spiders are known as bird-eating, whistling or barking spiders. They rub their pedipalps against their chelicerae to make a rasping sound which is rarely heard and is apparently made when the spiders are in their burrows.

DESCRIPTION: This spider's body and legs are grey-brown to dark brown. Males have a slimmer body and relatively longer legs than females.

LIFE HISTORY: The burrow of the adult may be 60 cm deep and the entrance is surrounded by a sheet of silk to trap prey. They feed on ground-dwelling insects and small vertebrates. Males are often seen during summer wandering in search of females, sometimes entering houses. The female constructs a white, oval egg sac about 35 mm long and 30 mm wide in her burrow, containing 45–50 yellow eggs. After the spiderlings hatch they remain with the female for some time, then disperse when about 10 mm in length and set up tiny burrows nearby.

BEHAVIOUR: This species is active at night. Outside the burrow it will flee when disturbed but defend itself when cornered by rearing up and striking downwards with its fangs.

HABITAT: Found in wet and dry forests, rainforests and woodlands. Burrows are usually dug into the upper banks of creeks and rivers.

VENOM: With fangs almost 1 cm long, this species can give a painful bite. The venom may cause nausea and vomiting but has no lasting effects.

DISTRIBUTION: Qld and NT.

SIZE: Male body length 55 mm, female 60 mm.

Inset: The female is more stout-bodied with shorter legs than the male.

The Sydney Funnelweb Spider is just one of a number of funnelweb species in Australia but is one of the best known spiders in the world due to its incredibly potent venom. The venom of this spider killed fifteen people before an antivenom was developed in the 1980s.

DESCRIPTION: The abdomen is dark brown to black with a thick covering of short hairs. The cephalothorax and legs are glossy black. Males are slimmer than females with longer, thinner legs.

LIFE HISTORY: Mating takes place in the female's burrow, after which the female produces a single white egg sac containing up to 120 eggs. The spiderlings may remain in the burrow for many months before dispersing to dig their own burrows, usually following rain. The burrow of an adult, situated under a log or stone, may be up to 30 cm deep.

BEHAVIOUR: Females rarely leave their burrows unless they become flooded, but males venture out in search of a female during summer. When disturbed, the male will raise his body up and strike down repeatedly with his fangs.

HABITAT: Found in woodlands, dry forests and suburban areas.

VENOM: This species is considered by many to be the most dangerous spider in the world. Following a bite, severe symptoms may begin within ten minutes and death may occur in as little as fifteen minutes.

DISTRIBUTION: New South Wales, found only within about 150 km of the Sydney region.

SIZE: Male body length 25–30 mm, female 35–40 mm.

Advanced Spiders
Order: Araneomorphs

More than 100 million years after the first primitive spiders appeared, new types of spiders began to evolve. These new species were not restricted to living in burrows in damp locations. These were the first advanced spiders (Araneomorphs), which had several adaptations enabling them to colonise new habitats, particularly in the tree tops. Because of the wondrous array of insect prey available to them, the advanced spiders flourished and multiplied.

By far the largest and most conspicuous group of spiders, the advanced spiders are sometimes colourful and often bizarre in shape. Because their fangs work against each other like pincers and they do not need to strike downwards on their prey like primitive spiders (Mygalomorphs), they can hunt on unstable surfaces such as leaves and even flimsy webs.

Another important adaptation is the way advanced spiders breathe. Primitive spiders breathe through "book lungs" — two pairs of chambers underneath the abdomen filled with gill-like layers in the shape of a book. Book lungs work effectively only in moist environments. Advanced spiders developed spiracles similar to insects — small holes in the body through which air enters and which can be closed off to prevent moisture escaping. This adaptation meant they were no longer restricted to damp environments and were free to radiate across the landscape.

Top: Web spinning is a characteristic of advanced spiders and has been developed into an art form by the orb-weavers. **Right:** The bodies of advanced spiders have been modified into a range of shapes and colours, often designed to blend in with their backgrounds. **Opposite:** Six-spined Spider (*Austracantha minax*).

House Spiders
Family: Desidae

Black House Spider *Badumna insignis*

These native spiders frequently enter houses and build messy webs in window corners, where they may live for several years if allowed. This has given them their alternative common name of "Window Spiders".

DESCRIPTION: Males are similar to females but with relatively longer legs. Members of this species are often mistaken for funnelweb spiders.

LIFE HISTORY: The web comprises a funnel-like retreat fanning from a corner out to an irregular series of radiating threads joined by a messy lattice of silk. The female produces white, mound-shaped egg sacs in the retreat of her web and she guards them until they hatch and disperse by ballooning. These spiders feed on any small invertebrates, especially other spiders, that come into contact with their web. The female matures after one year and may live several years, remaining in the same web throughout her life. The male leaves his web to mate with the female in her retreat and they may stay together for some time after mating. He dies soon after.

BEHAVIOUR: Adults hide in their retreat during the day, becoming active at night.

HABITAT: Found in dry forest, woodlands and suburban areas. They commonly enter sheds and houses and prefer the corners of window sills.

VENOM: The bite may cause pain, muscular spasms and sweating, with no lasting effects. Despite their abundance, bites are rare because the spiders are shy and retiring.

DISTRIBUTION: All States and Territories.

SIZE: Male body length 9–12 mm, female 16–20 mm.

Top, left: When disturbed, Black House Spiders disappear in an instant into their webs.

Net-casting Spiders
Family: Deinopidae

Net-Casting Spider *Deinopis subrufa*

Net-casting Spiders demonstrate one of the most remarkable prey catching techniques in the animal kingdom, building small nets to ensnare passing insects.

DESCRIPTION: The male has a narrower body and slightly longer legs than the female (pictured, bottom). The male also has dark bands on the back of the body that are generally absent in females. This species ranges in colour from pale yellow to almost black. Because of their large eyes, they are also known as Ogre-faced Spiders.

LIFE HISTORY: The female builds a round egg sac, about 10 mm across, containing 120–220 eggs. After hatching, the spiderlings live in groups for about three weeks, before dispersing to live alone. They feed on a range of insects and catch them using a small rectangular net (pictured, below) made from highly expandable sticky silk, which is thrown over any passing prey that comes within reach. They also construct a web comprising a few non-sticky strands from which the spider hangs. Both sexes mature during summer. Courtship takes place by the male approaching the female's web and tweaking threads at the edge until she is ready.

BEHAVIOUR: During the day, Net-casting Spiders remain motionless amongst foliage. They are active at night.

HABITAT: Found in dry forests, woodlands, heathlands and suburban areas.

VENOM: This species has not been known to bite.

DISTRIBUTION: All States and Territories.

SIZE: Male body length 12–18 mm, female 20–25 mm.

Humped Spiders
Family: Uloboridae

Communal Humped Spider   *Uloborus congregabilis*

Humped spiders belong to the only family of spiders that does not possess venom glands. They trap small flying insects in their incomplete orb webs and rapidly wrap their prey in silk to subdue it.

DESCRIPTION: The Communal Humped Spider's body and legs are pale grey to pale brown, with both lighter and darker markings. Males are similar to females (pictured, bottom) but almost half the size, with a more cylindrical abdomen.

LIFE HISTORY: The female constructs a flat, irregularly star-shaped egg sac, 6–12 mm in diameter, containing 15–30 pinkish eggs. The egg sac is attached to the web and guarded by the female until the eggs hatch; together the spider and sac appear as a small dried leaf caught in the web. The spiderlings hatch within a few weeks and remain in the web for some time before either dispersing or setting up webs at the edge of the female's web. They mature in late summer to autumn.

BEHAVIOUR: This species builds small orb webs in colonies made up of many spiders covering a large area, with intertwining support threads. They feed on small insects caught in the web. The webs are found in cool, dry sheltered areas both around humans and out in the bush.

HABITAT: Found in dry forest, woodland and suburban areas.

VENOM: This species does not possess venom glands.

DISTRIBUTION: NSW, Vic.

SIZE: Male body length 3 mm, female 4–6 mm.

Left and below: Humped spiders are well-named; The hump of the abdomen is several times taller than the rest of the body.

Daddy Long-legs
Family: Pholcidae

Daddy Long-legs *Pholcus phalangioides*

This is one of the best known spiders in the world due to its habit of living inside houses. Contrary to popular belief, Daddy Long-legs do not have venom capable of harming humans in any way.

DESCRIPTION: The body is pale cream to light brown, occasionally with darker markings on the legs and abdomen. Males have smaller bodies and longer legs than females.

LIFE HISTORY: The female produces a bundle of cream-coloured eggs held together with a few strands of silk and carried around in her fangs. After hatching, the spiderlings remain with the female for a few days before dispersing to build their own webs. The web is a thin tangled array of silk, up to 30 cm in diameter, and the spider uses it as a scaffold to throw silk over small insects, slaters and other spiders that venture near. They live in corners or dark spaces such as cupboards and behind furniture. In the bush they are found in tree hollows and caves.

BEHAVIOUR: Daddy Long-legs remain within the web but actively capture prey both at night and during the day.

HABITAT: While most common in and around houses, they are also found in dry forest and woodland areas.

VENOM: Despite the general belief that Daddy Long-legs are toxic, they are harmless and cause only a local reaction if anything.

DISTRIBUTION: Australia-wide.

SIZE: Male body length 5–6 mm, female 7–8 mm.

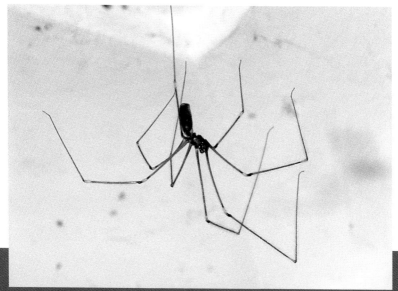

Wolf Spiders
Family: Lycosidae

Wolf spiders are a family of small to medium-sized spiders which are generally grey or brown with a striking series of dark brown or black markings on the body. The cephalothorax and abdomen are generally the same size, but the cephalothorax is high in front with prominent eyes.

Wolf spiders are found in a wide range of habitats, from coastal high tide lines to mountain tops. They are particularly common in semi-arid areas and survive well in deserts. This family of spiders is most notable for its range of interesting behaviours. Most species dig burrows in soft ground with their tough chelicerae. The burrow may be capped with a trapdoor, sheet web or collar of leaf litter around the entrance.

Wolf spiders are vagrant hunters, foraging for prey on the ground or amongst low foliage. They pounce on any ground-dwelling invertebrates, particularly insects, but also hunt prey larger than themselves. Prey is consumed on the spot before the spider resumes hunting. There are about 140 species of wolf spiders in Australia and more than 2300 worldwide.

Below: Like all wolf spider species, the Garden Wolf Spider has the front of the cephalothorax raised to accommodate the large eyes.

This species is probably the most common and well-known wolf spider in Australia. It is the largest ground-dwelling spider most people will see and is usually encountered in the backyard.

DESCRIPTION: Garden Wolf Spiders are generally pale brown to grey with darker brown and black markings. Adult males and females are similar in appearance.

LIFE HISTORY: During summer, the female constructs a flat, round, white egg sac about 10 mm in diameter. The egg sac is guarded by the female in the burrow and after about a month the spiderlings hatch and climb onto the back of the female's abdomen where they live for some time before dispersing to dig their own burrows. The burrow is decorated at the entrance with small leaves, twigs and bark. An adult's burrow may be 15–20 cm deep. The spider will sit at the entrance (as pictured, bottom) awaiting ground-dwelling invertebrates, although they will also leave the burrow and wander in search of prey.

BEHAVIOUR: These spiders are fast-moving and cover large distances when searching for prey. They are most active at night.

HABITAT: Found in dry and wet forests, woodlands, heathlands and suburban areas.

VENOM: This species is not aggressive but the bite is said to be painful, causing only local pain and swelling. There is some evidence that the bite can cause skin lesions in some people.

DISTRIBUTION: Qld, NSW, Vic, SA, WA.

SIZE: Male body length 18 mm, female 25 mm.

Top and below: The prominent eyes of wolf spiders are a distinguishing feature.

Desert Wolf Spider *Lycosa bicolor*

This species is active at night and males in particular can be fast moving and strongly defensive when disturbed. However, if near its burrow, the spider will retreat rather than turn on an attacker. The effect of the Desert Wolf Spider's bite is not known.

DESCRIPTION: The abdomen is black with a yellow-brown stripe along the length, which varies in width. The cephalothorax is yellow-brown and the eyes black.

LIFE HISTORY: Very little is known of the biology of this species. The spiders live in burrows 10–25 cm deep, depending on the soil type, with an entrance up to 15 mm in diameter, depending on the age and size of the spider. These burrows are constructed in red sandy to clay soils in open areas, particularly in disturbed areas such as roadsides. There is no lid to the burrow and the spider sits just below the opening at night, with its front legs and part of its body protruding out, awaiting passing prey. Desert Wolf Spiders are found throughout the year but are most common during late spring and summer.

BEHAVIOUR: Adults shelter in their burrows during the day and are active at night, sitting at the entrance to the burrow or on the ground just outside.

HABITAT: Found in woodlands and shrublands in arid and semi-arid areas.

VENOM: The venom is not known but the spider should be treated with caution.

DISTRIBUTION: SA, WA, NT.

SIZE: Male body length 20 mm, female 24 mm.

Below: Desert Wolf Spiders protrude out of their burrow, awaiting passing prey.

Nursery Web Spiders
Family: Pisauridae

Nursery web spiders are a family very similar in appearance to wolf spiders but are distinguished by the arrangement of eyes. This family does not have enlarged eyes at the front of the head like wolf spiders and the cephalothorax is not raised.

HABITAT: Nursery web spiders are found in swampy areas, mangroves and around ponds and creeks. Many species are seen on the surface of ponds.

BEHAVIOUR: These spiders can be strongly defensive when disturbed and jump about rapidly. Much of their time is spent immobile on the water surface with their legs splayed out. They do not dig a burrow or build a retreat, but females do construct a shelter (or "nursery") for their spiderlings when they are ready to hatch.

WEB: Nursery web spiders do not build a web.

FEEDING HABITS: These spiders are vagrant hunters, foraging for prey in and around water bodies. They feed on aquatic insects as well as fish, tadpoles and frogs.

BREEDING: The female may carry the egg sac while hunting, but instead of attaching it to the back of the abdomen, she carries it underneath the body, held in place by the chelicerae and a few strands of silk from the spinnerets.

NO. OF SPECIES: There are about 35 species of nursery web spiders in Australia and more than 300 species worldwide.

SIZE: Body length 7–25 mm.

Top: Sitting on a rock at the edge of a creek at night, these spiders are never far from water. **Below:** Nursery web spiders are able to skate across the surface of a pond with remarkable skill and speed.

Cell Spiders
Family: Dysderidae

Slater-eating Spider *Dysdera crocata*

For a number of years, this species was thought to be an Australian native. It is however, introduced from Europe and has spread to many parts of the world including New Zealand, America and Japan, where its favourite food source, slaters, have also been introduced.

DESCRIPTION: This is a distinctive species with a cream to yellow abdomen that has a silvery sheen produced by a very fine covering of hairs. The cephalothorax and legs are reddish-brown and the chelicerae greatly enlarged. The male is slimmer and slightly smaller than the female.

LIFE HISTORY: The female constructs a retreat of tough white silk under stones or at the base of a plant in which, after mating, she makes an egg sac. The egg sac contains up to 40 cream coloured eggs. The spiderlings disperse soon after hatching.

BEHAVIOUR: Adults shelter in moist areas under rocks, around plants or in piles of garden waste. They wander at night in search of slaters and their front pair of legs are thought to be specifically adapted for this purpose. Adults can be found during summer and autumn.

HABITAT: Suburban areas where slaters are found.

VENOM: There are reports of the bite of this species causing nausea, fever and severe swelling around the site of the bite, with victims taking several days to recover.

DISTRIBUTION: NSW, Vic, SA, Tas.

SIZE: Male body length 10 mm, female 15 mm.

Right: Slaters — this spider's food source, are also an introduced species.

Lynx Spiders
Family: Oxyopidae

Lynx spiders are a family of small spiders, characterised by a series of long spines arising at right angles from long legs. Their bodies are usually narrow and cylindrical with stripes and other patterns (usually pale green and yellow) that help them to blend in with their background.

HABITAT: Lynx spiders are found in a wide range of habitats such as grasslands, woodlands, dry forest and suburban areas.

BEHAVIOUR: These spiders are found on foliage and appear to have no trouble clinging to leaves being blown in the wind. They are active in bright sunshine and will leap considerable distances after prey. When resting, the spider will press its body against a leaf and be remarkably well camouflaged. They do not build a shelter, even in which to moult or lay eggs.

WEB: Lynx spiders do not build a web to catch prey.

FEEDING HABITS: Lynx spiders are active hunters and have excellent vision, due to their eyes being directed in front of their bodies.

Below: Some lynx spiders are more stout-bodied than other species and many are attractively patterned.

BREEDING: Mating usually takes place on foliage. The female constructs an egg sac which she deposits in a rolled leaf bound at the edges with a few strands of silk.

NO. OF SPECIES: There are fifteen species of lynx spiders in Australia and about 430 worldwide.

SIZE: Body length 5–9 mm.

Above: A female Lynx Spider guarding her egg sac. The sac is contained in a loosely rolled leaf, bound with silk.

Ant Spiders
Family: Zodariidae

Common Ant Spider *Storena formosa*

Ant spiders are so called due to their habit of running rapidly across the ground like an ant, changing direction frequently. Although they have the warning colours of contrasting red and black, they do not appear to be venomous.

DESCRIPTION: The Common Ant Spider's abdomen is black with five large spots varying in colour from cream to yellow. The cephalothorax and legs of the female (pictured, below) are bright red but the front half and the chelicerae are black. In males, the front half of the body is completely black. There are more than 100 species of ant spiders in Australia, but this species is the most colourful.

LIFE HISTORY: Very little is known about the biology of this species. The female constructs an egg sac in a shallow depression under a log or stone and stays with it until the eggs hatch. During the day, adults shelter under logs in silken retreats made of small twigs and dead leaves.

BEHAVIOUR: At night they roam in search of prey, hiding amongst leaf litter when disturbed. They are sometimes found near ant hills so may feed on foraging ants. They appear to feed mostly on nocturnal ground-dwelling insects such as crickets.

HABITAT: Found in dry forests, woodlands and semi-arid regions.

VENOM: This species is not known to bite.

DISTRIBUTION: Qld, NSW, Vic, SA, WA.

SIZE: Male body length 12 mm, female 16 mm.

Clubionid Spiders
Family: Clubionidae

Robust Clubionid Spider   *Clubiona robusta*

Of the dozen or more species of clubionid spiders in Australia, this attractive species is by far the most common and widespread. It does not venture into houses but is regularly seen in gardens and roaming tree trunks in bushland.

DESCRIPTION: The abdomen is dark cream in colour with a solid reddish-brown stripe down the centre and similar stripes down the sides. The fine hairs covering the cylindrical abdomen give it a slightly silky appearance. The cephalothorax is more reddish-pink and the chelicerae are dark crimson to black. The legs vary in colour from pale cream to pinkish brown. The male has a slimmer abdomen than the female.

LIFE HISTORY: The female (pictured, below) constructs a silken retreat under bark, up to 5 cm long, which she uses as a moulting chamber during development and also as a brood chamber after mating. The egg sac is about 1 cm in diameter and contains up to 150 cream-coloured eggs. The spiderlings disperse soon after hatching.

BEHAVIOUR: Adults can be seen roaming around bark at night, feeding on other spiders as well as beetles, bugs and moths. Occasionally this species also hunts amongst foliage. They spend the day inside the retreat under bark. Adults are most commonly seen from November to April.

HABITAT: Found in woodlands, dry forests and suburban areas.

VENOM: This species is not known to bite.

DISTRIBUTION: All States and Territories.

SIZE: Male body length 13 mm, female 20 mm.

Top: The large, dark chelicerae and characteristic arrangement of eyes are clearly visible on this spider.

Miturgid Spiders
Family: Miturgidae

Sac Spider *Cheiracanthium mordax*

Australia has become home to a great number of introduced invertebrate species, many of which are pests, including a number of spiders. Sac Spiders are one of the few Australian spider species that have been accidentally exported to other countries.

DESCRIPTION: The female is pale brown with a cream-coloured abdomen and a dark stripe down the back. The male is slightly darker. The male can also be distinguished by his remarkably long jaws (chelicerae).

LIFE HISTORY: The female constructs an egg sac in foliage and guards it until the eggs hatch. The spiderlings are vagrant hunters, feeding on any small, moving prey. During the day, the spiders hide in a silken retreat, usually made of leaves sewn together, but it may also be made under bark or behind furniture inside houses. They do not build a web to catch prey. Adults are most commonly found from November to March. Mating appears to take place inside the female's retreat and males and females are often found together.

BEHAVIOUR: Sac Spiders are active at night, roaming over foliage. They can be fast moving when disturbed. At night they hide inside the silken retreat.

HABITAT: Found in dry forests, woodlands and suburban areas. This species is also called the Common Garden Leaf Spider as it is regularly found in gardens.

VENOM: The bite may cause local pain and ulceration, nausea and headache.

DISTRIBUTION: NSW, ACT, Vic, Tas.

SIZE: Male body length 9 mm, female 10 mm.

Left: These spiders do a commendable job in the garden controlling caterpillars and other garden pests.

The colour of the adult Lined Miturga varies from light to dark brown and grey, always with four white stripes on the undersurface of the abdomen. They are ground-dwelling spiders that live and hunt amongst grass tussocks.

DESCRIPTION: Lined Miturgas are similar in appearance to wolf spiders but can be distinguished by the four white stripes underneath. Males are similar in colour, pattern and shape to females but smaller and slimmer.

LIFE HISTORY: Adults construct a retreat of thick white silk close to or on the ground, usually amongst grass or tussocks or under fallen bark. The retreat, which may be up to 15 cm long, is bag-shaped with several openings. The female constructs several mound-shaped, oval to round white egg sacs, about 15 mm in diameter, which are attached to the inner wall of her retreat. The sac contains up to 100 eggs. These spiders feed on a variety of ground-dwelling insects.

BEHAVIOUR: This species is active at night and shelters in its retreat during the day. If the retreat is disturbed, the spider moves rapidly out through one of the openings and hides in the grass, where it is almost undetectable. It can also run fast over open areas at night.

HABITAT: Found in dry forest, woodland and semi-arid areas.

VENOM: The fangs of this species are large and the bite may be painful. It may cause headaches, nausea and vomiting.

DISTRIBUTION: NSW, Vic, SA.

SIZE: Male body length 11 mm, female 20 mm.

Top, right: Lined Miturga spiderlings not yet emerged from their egg sac.

Swift Spiders
Family: Corinnidae

Common Swift Spiders   *Supunna* spp.

The extremely fast-moving species of swift spiders are found only in the Australian region. When hunting, these spiders press their bodies to the ground with legs spread flat, making it difficult to see them against pebbles or leaf litter. If prey comes within range, the spider races off almost faster than the eye can follow.

DESCRIPTION: Adults have black bodies with white stripes, spots and other white markings. There are at least seven species in the genus. Some, like the Spotted Ground Swift Spider (*Supunna picta*, pictured, below) have reddish-orange forelegs, while others have black and white legs.

LIFE HISTORY: The female constructs a flat, white egg sac under bark, a log or a flat stone. The eggs may be attacked by parasitic wasps. Little else is known of the life history of swift spiders.

BEHAVIOUR: Common swift spiders hunt along the ground for insects and other invertebrates. They move particularly rapidly in hot weather and stop frequently to hide amongst leaf litter, then move off and change direction mid-flight without warning. Although they hunt mostly on the ground, they will also climb walls in search of prey. Some species wave their front legs in the air as they run, giving them the appearance of a ground wasp.

HABITAT: Found in woodlands, dry forest, semi-arid and suburban areas.

VENOM: Not known to bite.

DISTRIBUTION: Qld, NSW, Vic, NT.

SIZE: Male body length 5–9 mm, female 6–12 mm.

Ground Spiders
Family: Lamponidae

White-tailed Spider *Lampona cylindrata*

This is one of the most feared spiders in Australia and is the cause of some hysteria. But while many people believe White-tailed Spider venom to be very toxic, there is little evidence to support this and reactions to bites range from no reaction at all to local blistering.

DESCRIPTION: Juveniles and adult males have a pattern of white marks on the abdomen, but females (pictured, bottom) have a single white spot which fades with age.

LIFE HISTORY: The female constructs a circular white egg sac about 10 mm in diameter, which contains 50–100 pink eggs. The spiderlings emerge after about two months and remain close to their mother for about a week, living under a communal sheet web. They then disperse and prey on insects and other spiders, particularly the Black House Spider (*Badumna insignis*). White-tailed Spiders are vagrants and do not build a web of their own, catching prey as they wander at night. During the day they hide under bark or rocks, or behind cupboards and under furniture in houses.

BEHAVIOUR: This species is generally slow moving but can run rapidly when disturbed. They are active at night.

HABITAT: Found in woodlands and suburban areas.

VENOM: Bites from this species are relatively common, due to their habit of wandering inside houses and hiding during the day in shoes, clothing and bedding. Symptoms may include local blistering around the bite site and nausea.

DISTRIBUTION: All States and Territories.

SIZE: Male body length 15 mm, female 18 mm.

Top: Juvenile White-tailed Spiders are attractively patterned. **Below:** White-tailed Spiders capture their prey as they wander at night.

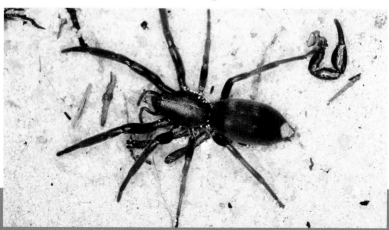

Flat Spiders
Family: Gnaphosidae

Rebilus Flat Spider   *Rebilus* spp.

There are at least five species of fast-moving rebilus flat spiders in Australia. As their name suggests, they have incredibly flattened bodies, superbly adapted to squeeze into the smallest gaps in bark or under flat rocks.

DESCRIPTION: The body is generally chocolate brown but the cephalothorax may be considerably darker, tending to black. The legs are reddish brown and held out flat to the sides of the body. Depending on the species, darker lines or dimples may be present on the top surface of the abdomen. The most common and widespread member of the genus is a species (*Rebilus castaneus*) from Western Australia.

LIFE HISTORY: After mating, the female constructs a very flat, white egg sac in a sheltered position such as under bark or a slab of rock. The smooth, round egg sac measures about 20 mm in diameter and contains up to 50 cream-coloured eggs. Little else is known of this spider's life history.

BEHAVIOUR: Unlike related species which build a silken retreat in the same situations, rebilus flat spiders are vagrant hunters and only build shelters to moult or lay eggs in. They feed on a range of insects and spiders.

HABITAT: Found in heathlands, woodlands and dry forests.

VENOM: Rebilus flat spiders will defend themselves when disturbed and are known to give a painful bite with no lasting symptoms.

DISTRIBUTION: East coast and west coast of Australia.

SIZE: Male body length 9–12 mm, female 15–17 mm.

Top: The rebilus flat spider may be seen patrolling tree trunks at night in search of prey.

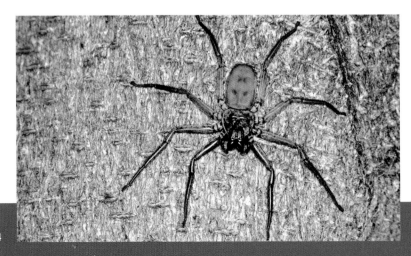

Two-tailed Spiders

Family: Hersiliidae

Two-tailed Spiders are a group of small to medium-sized spiders that are rarely seen due to their astonishingly effective camouflage. They have flattened bodies and long legs but the most distinctive feature is the pair of long spinnerets which extend beyond the end of the abdomen.

HABITAT: Two-tailed Spiders are found in heavily forested areas, particularly in tropical and subtropical areas. Some species occur in arid areas and are absent from Tasmania.

BEHAVIOUR: These spiders spend almost all of their time sitting flat against the bark of a tree. When disturbed, they run rapidly around to the other side of the tree. When on the move, the spider lifts its spinnerets up to avoid damaging them on the bark.

WEB: Two-tailed Spiders do not build webs to catch prey.

FEEDING HABITS: Two-tailed Spiders are ambush predators, lying in wait for insect prey then running around it in circles, swathing it in broad sheets of silk before feeding. This happens so fast it is almost a blur.

BREEDING: Mating presumably takes place on bark and the female constructs a flat silken egg sac which she guards until the eggs hatch. The spiderlings remain with her for some time before dispersing.

NO. OF SPECIES: There are more than 50 species of Two-tailed Spiders in Australia and over 100 species worldwide.

SIZE: Body length 3–8 mm.

Right: An adult female Two-tailed Spider guarding her egg sac. She will not abandon it, even when threatened.

Jumping Spiders
Family: Salticidae

A very large family of small spiders featuring bodies clothed with fine scales. These scales come in a remarkable range of colours and give many species a brilliant iridescent sheen. Jumping spiders are common in backyards and are frequently seen foraging during the day. The front pair of eyes may be greatly enlarged and the pedipalps of many species appear "furry" due to the covering of white hairs. Body length ranges from 4–15 mm. Because the family is so large and diverse, it is found in a great variety of habitats, from grasslands and dry woodlands to tropical rainforests.

Jumping spiders have excellent vision and are active during the day, stalking prey around foliage and tree trunks. They do not build webs but leap onto prey from 10 cm away or more. When leaping, they leave behind a silken safety line attached to a leaf. If the spider misses its prey, it swings down on the end of the safety line and climbs back up to try again.

Mating is often preceded by elaborate courtship dances involving both sexes. The male is often brilliantly coloured and he angles his body to present himself to the female in the best possible light. After mating, the female produces an egg sac which is hidden in a curled leaf bound with silk or under bark.

This is the largest family of spiders in the world. There are about 380 species of jumping spiders in Australia and more than 5000 species worldwide.

Top: Jumping Spiders such as *Holoplatys* spp. have wide, flattened bodies, well suited to living under bark.

This species bears a strong resemblance to its ant prey in many areas of its range, suggesting a relationship that may involve visual and perhaps other forms of mimicry. It is one of a number of jumping spider species which may be specifically adapted to capturing ants.

DESCRIPTION: A black spider with a distinctive gold band around the abdomen. Males are similar in colour, pattern and shape to females, but their gold band is brighter.

LIFE HISTORY: The female constructs a circular egg sac 5–6 mm in diameter, containing 25–40 dark cream-coloured eggs. The egg sac is produced in the female's retreat. The spiderlings disperse to catch their own prey, mainly ants, small insects and other spiders. The spiders mature in early summer. They hunt for prey around the bark of gum trees and other native trees, moving rapidly and leaping on prey from some distance. Females construct a silken retreat under bark, 15–25 mm long and 10 mm wide, in which she shelters and constructs her egg sac.

BEHAVIOUR: Adults can be fast moving when necessary, but spend considerable periods resting. They are active throughout the day, particularly on sunny days.

HABITAT: Found mostly in dry forests and woodlands, but also common in gardens. It usually hides under the bark of gum trees.

VENOM: This species is not known to bite.

DISTRIBUTION: All States and Territories.

SIZE: Male body length 7 mm, female 9 mm.

Peacock Jumping Spider _Cosmophasis micarioides_

This is one of Australia's more colourful species of spider. Adults are brilliantly decorated with red, blue, orange, yellow and white. Because of its small size, it can be easy to miss when foraging on foliage, but close inspection reveals the iridescent patterns.

DESCRIPTION: The legs are banded with black and white. Males and females are very similar to each other.

LIFE HISTORY: Young spiders and adults feed on insects caught on foliage and their prey is often bigger than they are. They are active during the day and can be seen when sunlight reveals their colours as they hunt amongst foliage. At night or during rainy periods the spider hides under leaves. They are preyed upon by ants and other spiders. Like many other Australian spider species, particularly jumping spiders, little detail is known of the life history of the Peacock Jumping Spider.

BEHAVIOUR: Both adults and juveniles are active spiders which can be seen moving rapidly around foliage. When standing still, the spider rapidly waves its hairy white pedipalps at the front of the body. During courtship, the male undertakes an elaborate dance for the female.

HABITAT: Found in tropical rainforests. This species is found on some islands in the Pacific, suggesting they are able to balloon there as spiderlings and can establish wherever there is suitable habitat.

VENOM: This species is not known to bite.

DISTRIBUTION: North-eastern Qld.

SIZE: Adult body length 9–10 mm.

This species lives a particularly dangerous life — venturing inside the nests of Green Tree Ants to feed on the larvae. Unlike other spiders associated with Green Tree Ants, this species does not mimic the ant in shape or colour, but is thought to mimic the smell of the ants.

DESCRIPTION: Adults and juveniles are orange or copper coloured all over, with lines of silvery blue edged with black. Males are similar to females.

LIFE HISTORY: The eggs are laid by the female either on or inside the outer chambers of a Green Tree Ant nest. The spiders feed on a range of insects, and will eat members of its own species, but mostly eat Green Tree Ant grubs. They enter nests and prey on grubs left unattended, as well as grubs being transported between nests. The spider approaches an ant worker carrying a grub and touches the ant's antennae with its front legs in a way that encourages the ant to release the grub.

BEHAVIOUR: Both males and females are active spiders. Males undertake a spectacular courtship dance in the presence of females, moving rapidly back and forth with the body raised high off the ground and the abdomen pointing vertically.

HABITAT: Found in a range of habitats where Green Tree Ants occur, particularly tropical rainforest.

VENOM: This species is not known to bite.

DISTRIBUTION: Eastern Queensland.

SIZE: Adult body length 9–10 mm.

This colourful species is probably Australia's largest jumping spider. The male (pictured, bottom) has a large tuft of white hairs on each side of his "face" and a pointed top-knot of black hair above the eyes, giving him a distinctively regal appearance.

DESCRIPTION: The eyes of the female are surrounded by a pattern of bright red and white, while males are darker and slimmer. The first pair of legs are longer than the other pairs and are dark brown to black.

LIFE HISTORY: The female constructs a shelter between leaves woven together with silk and inside she produces a white, disc-shaped egg sac, about 30 mm in diameter, containing 60–80 yellow eggs. The spiderlings remain with the female for some time after hatching, then disperse to begin a vagrant life hunting insects and other spiders. They are most often seen stalking through foliage after prey and can leap gaps of more than 15 cm. Both adults and juveniles can overpower prey much larger than themselves.

BEHAVIOUR: This species is most active during the day but can also be seen roaming at night for prey. Males undergo an elaborate courtship display.

HABITAT: Found in a range of habitats, from rainforest to suburban areas.

VENOM: There are reports of painful bites from this species resulting in a slow-healing ulcer-like sore which leaves no permanent mark.

DISTRIBUTION: Qld, Northern NSW, NT.

SIZE: Male body length 12 mm, female 15 mm.

Left: The eyes of the female Northern Green Jumping Spider are surrounded by bright red and white markings.

This fairly drab jumping spider occurs along the eastern coast of Australia but is most common and widespread in New South Wales. It can be seen in many backyards, roaming tree trunks in search of prey during the day.

DESCRIPTION: The colour of both sexes ranges from red-brown to dark grey-brown. There is a distinctive black Y-shaped marking in the middle of the abdomen. The body is shorter and stouter than most species of jumping spiders. Males are very similar in colour, shape and pattern to the females, but the first pair of legs are longer in the male.

LIFE HISTORY: The female constructs an oval white egg sac, 10–12 mm in diameter, containing 35–50 pale brown eggs. The spiderlings live under the loose bark of gum trees and other native trees and sometimes roam on the outside of the bark.

BEHAVIOUR: They are very active spiders, feeding on insects such as cockroaches and booklice, as well as small spiders. If disturbed, the spider disappears rapidly under bark or drops to the ground where it is very difficult to see. Adult males and females are very well camouflaged and hunt around tree trunks. They are sometimes found together under bark.

HABITAT: Found in dry forests, woodlands and suburban areas.

VENOM: This species is not known to bite.

DISTRIBUTION: Qld, NSW, Vic, Tas.

SIZE: Male and female body length. 8–10 mm.

Huntsman Spiders

Family: Heteropodidae

Huntsmans are a family of medium to large spiders with flattened brown or grey bodies and legs that are turned sideways to enable the spider to fit into very narrow spaces. The first two pairs of legs are noticeably longer than the back two pairs. Males are usually slightly smaller than the females with distinctively large pedipalps. Body length varies from 15-45 mm. Huntsmans are found Australia-wide in a great range of habitats, particularly dry forests and woodlands. They are also common in suburban areas, rainforests and semi-arid regions.

Members of this family generally shelter during the day and emerge at night to feed. Some species dig a semi-permanent burrow in the ground but most construct shelters under bark or amongst dead leaves. They are fast moving when necessary but spend considerable periods resting. Huntsman spiders do not build a web for catching prey, but are active hunters and forage widely over bark and foliage looking for prey. Upon encountering an insect, the spider leaps upon it and feeds on the spot.

Before mating, many species undertake an elaborate courtship dance of many stages lasting a number of hours. Usually taking place under bark, courtship involves the male raising his body off the tree trunk and drumming the bark with his pedipalps. After mating, the female constructs a tough egg sac which she guards until the eggs hatch.

There are about 100 species of huntsmans in Australia and more than 1000 species worldwide.

Badge Spiders are distinctively orange huntsmans with a black, shield-shaped "badge" underneath the abdomen which gives the genus its common name. Unlike most huntsmans, Badge Spiders will rear up with fangs open to defend themselves when disturbed and can give a painful bite.

DESCRIPTION: This species is generally orange to pinkish-brown, but juveniles may be green. The shield underneath the abdomen is pitch black with white markings. Males are very similar to females.

LIFE HISTORY: The female constructs a flat white egg sac under bark which she guards. The greenish spiderlings emerge from the egg sac during spring and begin a vagrant life hunting insects and other invertebrates. During the day this species hides under the bark of trees or logs on the ground.

At night they roam foliage and tree trunks, occasionally entering houses. The spider builds a silken retreat under bark in which to moult and the female constructs a similar one in which to make her egg sac.

BEHAVIOUR: This species is active at night, moving amongst foliage and around tree trunks. It can be fast moving when disturbed.

HABITAT: Found in dry eucalypt forest and woodlands, as well as suburban areas, particularly bushy gardens.

VENOM: The bites of related species may cause severe local pain, sweating, nausea and vomiting. This species has been implicated in the death of a domestic cat.

DISTRIBUTION: NSW, Vic.

SIZE: Male body length 16 mm, female 20 mm.

This species is very common in the Sydney region and, like a number of Australian huntsmans, it often enters houses. It is sometimes called the Sydney Huntsman and is probably the largest huntsman in Australia, with a legspan of 160 mm or more.

DESCRIPTION: The body and legs are light greyish-white with dark brown to black bands and markings. Males are slimmer than females with longer legs.

LIFE HISTORY: The female constructs a flat, oval egg sac of white, papery silk, about 25 mm diameter, containing 200 green eggs. Upon hatching, the spiderlings emerge singly through a small hole in the egg sac created by their mother. The spiderlings disperse after their first moult by ballooning away to live under bark, logs and stones, feeding on small insects which they capture by running down. Adult spiders feed on larger insects such as beetles and moths. Mating takes place under bark with the pair facing each other and may be a lengthy process.

BEHAVIOUR: Most activity and feeding takes place at night, although they are occasionally active during the day.

HABITAT: Found in dry forests and some suburban areas. It is probably most common in the subtropical areas of eastern Australia, living under loose bark, large flat rocks, corrugated iron and within fibro walls.

VENOM: This species can give a painful bite but causes no other symptoms.

DISTRIBUTION: Qld, NSW, Vic.

SIZE: Male body length 30 mm, female 45 mm.

Left: The markings on the back of the Grey Huntsman Spider are variable. The black bands on the legs are the most striking feature.

Bark Huntsman Spider *Holconia montana*

Although this species naturally lives under bark and can often be seen roaming tree trunks at night, it may also enter houses. This is one of the most common spiders inside houses in southern Australia. In rural areas it is sometimes known as a "Triantelope".

DESCRIPTION: The Bark Huntsman Spider varies from brown to grey. Males and females are very similar but differ in size and the presence of enlarged pedipalps in the male. Dark bands may or may not be present on the legs of both sexes.

LIFE HISTORY: The female constructs a flat, oval egg sac of papery white silk under the bark of trees. The spiderlings remain with the eggs sac for some time after hatching, then disperse to begin a vagrant life on their own, hunting insects and other invertebrates. Adults

shelter during the day under the loose bark of gum trees and frequently enter cars and houses. Mating generally takes place under bark. Adults live about two years.

BEHAVIOUR: These huntsmans are active at night, moving slowly and steadily in search of prey. Because of their large size and rapid sideways movement when disturbed, they can cause alarm but are unaggressive.

HABITAT: Found in dry forest, woodland and suburban areas.

VENOM: The bite causes only local pain and swelling. Although this spider is common, bites are very rare because it is a shy species.

DISTRIBUTION: NSW, Vic.

SIZE: Male body length 20 mm, female 30 mm.

Brown Huntsman Spider *Heteropoda cervina*

Brown Huntsman Spiders are very common in the top half of eastern Australia and regularly enter houses where they feed on moths and flies. Despite their abundance, very little is known of their biology.

DESCRIPTION: The body is mid to dark brown with darker brown to black markings. The legs may be banded with paler brown and dark spots. The hairs on the legs are also variable in colour and abundance. Males are slightly slimmer than females with longer legs, but similar in colour and pattern.

LIFE HISTORY: Nothing is known of the mating behaviour or early stages of this species' life history. Adults shelter under bark during the day and roam at night in search of prey.

BEHAVIOUR: This species is very fast moving and will move in rapid jumps across open ground when seriously threatened. Adults are often seen on roads at night in some parts of their range. Adults have also been observed hanging from bark by the back two pairs of legs with the front two pairs dangling free, but the purpose of this behaviour is not known. They feed on other spiders and bark-dwelling insects such as caterpillars, crickets and moths.

HABITAT: Found in woodlands, dry forests and suburban areas.

VENOM: The bite of the Brown Huntsman Spider is said to be painful but there are no serious symptoms recorded.

DISTRIBUTION: Queensland, New South Wales.

SIZE: Male body length 20 mm, female 25 mm.

Crab Spiders
Family: Thomisidae

A very large family of small to medium-sized spiders, crab spiders are generally either grey, brown, white, yellow or green, depending on their way of life. Some species are brightly patterned whilst others are covered with hairs or tubercles which aid in camouflage. Body length varies from 4-14 mm. They are found mostly in tropical and subtropical areas, particularly in wet forest. There are far fewer species in southern Australia.

Members of this family spend most of the time sitting immobile on flowers, foliage or bark awaiting prey. They do not build a web to catch prey. Because of the arrangement of their legs, they move sideways when disturbed. Crab spiders have good eyesight and possess the unusual ability to move the front pair of eyes independently of each other.

Crab spiders are ambush predators, patiently lying in wait for prey. They sit with the first two pairs of legs spread wide, ready to grasp insects or other spiders that come within reach. If prey is scarce, the spider may release a long thread of silk and drift across to another location.

There is often a vast size difference between males and females of the same species. Following mating, the female constructs a whitish egg sac which she hides in a folded leaf sealed with a layer of silk.

This is one of the largest families of spiders. There are about 125 species of crab spiders in Australia and more than 2000 species worldwide.

Top, right: Most crab spider species are green to match plant foliage. **Below:** Crab Spiders characteristically sit with the front legs apart, awaiting passing prey.

This species is common in tropical Australia and is also present in Papua New Guinea, Indonesia and India. It commonly captures bees and wasps that unsuspectingly visit its flower, killing them instantly with a bite to the back of the neck.

DESCRIPTION: The female is large and white all over, with a translucent cephalothorax and legs. The male is tiny in comparison and has a rounder body than the female, ranging in colour from yellow through to orange and brown.

LIFE HISTORY: The female constructs a smooth white egg sac, about 15 mm in diameter, containing 200–400 cream-coloured eggs. Each egg is about 1 mm in diameter. These spiders sit on leaves or,

more commonly, on flowers and flowerheads, with their front pair of legs held wide open awaiting prey. The two front pairs of legs are longer than the other two pairs and are spined to improve grip on struggling prey. They feed on flying insect pollinators such as bees and butterflies, but will also prey on other species of spiders and ants.

BEHAVIOUR: Like most crab spiders, this species is slow moving and sits motionless during the day awaiting passing prey. It does not appear to hunt at night.

HABITAT: Found in dry forests, woodlands, heathlands and suburban areas.

VENOM: There are some unconfirmed reports of the bite of this species, but the symptoms are not serious.

DISTRIBUTION: Qld, Northern NSW, NT.

SIZE: Male body length 2–3 mm, female 12 mm.

Left: A White Crab Spider with a European Honeybee. The bee has been bitten on the back of the neck whilst visiting flowers.

These spiders vary considerably in colour, ranging from almost white to deep red, but the most common pattern is shown here (pictured, bottom). The long oval shape of the adult disguises it superbly whilst resting on grass heads, with front legs spread wide to capture passing prey.

DESCRIPTION: The cephalothorax has a broad brown band down each side, with a narrow brown stripe down the middle. The abdomen is deep orange-red with two clear cream stripes near the top. There are also two distinctive pits at the top of the abdomen. Although males are much smaller than females, their legs are about the same length.

LIFE HISTORY: The female constructs a very white, oval egg sac, about 10 mm in diameter, attached to seeding grass heads and covered with grass seeds and other debris. The female remains with the sac until the spiderlings hatch and will not abandon it even when severely disturbed. The egg sac contains 40–60 cream-coloured eggs. Adults are found from November to March.

BEHAVIOUR: This species is active during the day. Adults do not build webs but sit on grass heads with their front pair of legs wide apart, waiting for small insects such as moths attracted to the seeds.

HABITAT: Found in grasslands and some open forest.

VENOM: This species is not known to bite.

DISTRIBUTION: Qld, NSW, Vic.

SIZE: Male body length 4 mm, female 9 mm.

This species is very common in the backyards of southern Australia but almost nothing is known of its life history. It is very similar to, and often confused with, its close relative Sidymella longipes, *which occurs in backyards up the east coast.*

DESCRIPTION: A pale brown spider with a dark stripe down the cephalothorax. The characteristic feature is the trapezium-shaped abdomen. The abdomen of some specimens may be a darker brown than the rest of the body, the same colour as the stripe on the cephalothorax. The legs are the same colour as the body, with dark spots at irregular intervals and a series of spines on the inner surfaces. The male is smaller and slimmer than the female, with slightly longer legs.

LIFE HISTORY: Adults are usually found on grasses and low shrubs, sitting with their front two pairs of legs spread apart to catch prey. Nothing is known of their reproduction or life history, but the eggs are probably deposited in an egg sac hidden within a partially curled leaf.

BEHAVIOUR: Feeds on small insects and probably small spiders. Like all crab spiders, this species does not build a web and sits amongst foliage or flowerheads awaiting passing prey.

HABITAT: Found in woodlands and suburban areas.

VENOM: This species is not known to bite.

DISTRIBUTION: NSW, Vic, SA, WA.

SIZE: Male body length 4 mm, female 6 mm.

Bark spiders rest with their legs held tightly against their bodies, usually in cracks in the bark of a tree. Their bodies are covered with microscopic fragments of bark from the same tree, usually pushed into crevices in the exoskeleton, which blends them perfectly into their background.

DESCRIPTION: The abdomen and cephalothorax is usually dark brown or grey with black mottled markings. The colour of the spider generally matches the colour of the bark on which it is resting and is only visible when it moves. Spiders resting on burnt bark will have black fragments attached to their bodies. One species (*Stephanopis barbipes*) has a long row of bristles on its front pair of legs, the purpose for which is not known. There are probably more than 30 species of bark spiders in Australia.

LIFE HISTORY: After mating, the female constructs flattened egg sacs which are also camouflaged with fragments of bark and deposited in crevices in the tree trunk. The egg sac may contain up to 35 eggs. The spiderlings disperse to find their own locations for hunting prey; they mature in early summer.

BEHAVIOUR: Most species rest during the day on bark and forage over the trunk at night to capture other spiders and bark-dwelling insects.

HABITAT: Found in heathlands, woodlands, wet and dry forests.

VENOM: Bark spiders are not known to bite.

DISTRIBUTION: All States and Territories.

SIZE: Male body length 3–6 mm, female 4–8 mm.

Flower spiders sit within flowerheads with their back legs anchored to the petals and their two front pairs of legs open, awaiting passing prey. When a fly, bee or even a wasp lands on the flower, the spider grabs it and quickly bites it in the back of the neck, immediately immobilising it.

DESCRIPTION: The round abdomens of flower spiders are usually white or pale yellow, with patterns of green, pink or red. The cephalothorax may be translucent yellow or green, as are the long legs. There are more than 30 Australian species belonging to this group.

LIFE HISTORY: The flat, white egg sac is usually built by the female underneath a leaf or within a folded leaf. There are generally less than 40 eggs per sac and they take about two weeks to hatch.

BEHAVIOUR: Adults spend their time sitting immobile on the edge of a flower, awaiting prey such as flies, bees, plant bugs and even other spiders. Occasionally more than one flower spider may be seen hunting at the same flowerhead. The spider usually chooses flowers of similar colour to itself, remaining undetected by predators as well as prey.

HABITAT: Found in heathlands, woodlands, dry and wet forest, suburban areas.

VENOM: Flower spiders are not known to bite.

DISTRIBUTION: All States and Territories.

SIZE: Male body length 3–5 mm, female 4–8 mm.

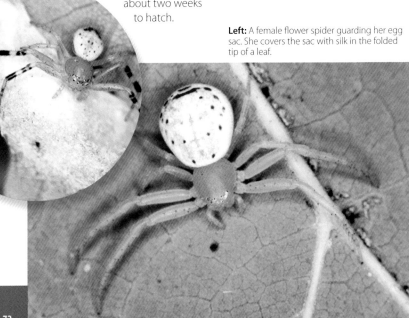

Left: A female flower spider guarding her egg sac. She covers the sac with silk in the folded tip of a leaf.

Leaf-rolling crab spiders are a group of small spiders which shelter in a retreat made from the tip of a leaf folded over twice and secured with silk. This protects them from some predators but not from parasitic wasps, which regularly lay their tiny white eggs on the outside of the spiders.

DESCRIPTION: Small crab spiders with round abdomens which are usually intricately patterned with dark lines and spots. There are at least seven species in Australia, each with a generally grey to brown abdomen and much darker cephalothorax. At least one species has a dark yellow abdomen.

LIFE HISTORY: Very little is known about the life history of these spiders. The egg sac, made of tough white silk, is built inside the female's shelter after mating and usually contains 30 eggs or fewer. Specimens are often seen with one or two eggs of a parasitic wasp on the cephalothorax which will hatch and eventually kill the spider, but occasionally a spider is covered with many eggs and neither the spider nor the wasps survive.

BEHAVIOUR: Adults remain inside the shelter during the day and emerge at night to feed on small flying insects.

HABITAT: Found in dry and wet forests, woodlands and rainforest. Most species prefer shady areas overhanging creeks and gullies.

VENOM: Leaf-rolling crab spiders are not known to bite.

DISTRIBUTION: Qld, NSW, Vic.

SIZE: Male body length 3–5 mm, female 4–8 mm.

Orb-weavers
Family: Araneidae

Orb-weavers are a large family of diverse spiders, united mainly by the presence of a pair of false claws in addition to the true claws at the ends of the legs. These false claws are thought to be involved in manipulating silk. Otherwise, members of this family demonstrate a great range of body shape, size and colour. Body length varies from 2–50 mm. They are found in just about every Australian habitat, but are least common in arid areas.

Orb-weavers demonstrate possibly the widest range of behaviours of any spider family. Some species actively hunt amongst foliage, others are ambushers and many sit in the hub of the orb web day and night. Members of this family are best known for their magnificent orb webs, but many species build poor webs or none at all.

Most species feed on prey trapped in the web, but a range of other prey catching techniques are employed. Triangular spiders (*Arcys* species) ambush prey on foliage and behave more like crab spiders and the Bird-Dropping Spider (*Celaenia excavata*) mimics female moth pheromones to lure male moths to their deaths.

Courtship, mating, egg laying and the type and location of egg sac also varies markedly between species. In some species, males and females are of equal size but in many the male is less than one hundredth the size of the female. These include some of the largest Australian spiders.

There are about 260 species of Orb-weavers in Australia and more than 2800 species worldwide.

Triangular Spider   *Arcys clavatus*

This spider is one of at least nine species of triangular spiders in Australia. All have triangular bodies, as their common name suggests and they are spectacularly patterned in bright orange with black markings and white spots.

DESCRIPTION: Males and females of this species are very similar in shape colour and pattern, although the female tends to have a broader abdomen. Because of their unusual colour and shape, they are usually not recognised as spiders at all.

LIFE HISTORY: In late summer, the female produces a cream-coloured, pear-shaped egg sac, suspended by strong threads from foliage. The sac is about 10 mm long and contains 50 yellow eggs. Very little is known about their life history and biology.

BEHAVIOUR: Triangular Spiders spend most of their time motionless on foliage, waiting for passing prey. They may remain in this position both day and night. The spider sits on leaves with its front pair of legs, which are lined with long spines, widely separated awaiting prey. When a small insect such as a moth, fly or lace bug comes within reach, the spider grabs the prey with a sudden swift movement. They regularly move between branches, playing out silk so they can cross large gaps.

HABITAT: Found in a range of habitats, but mostly dry forest. They are commonly found on regrowth plants after bushfires.

VENOM: This species has been known to bite but the symptoms are not serious.

DISTRIBUTION: Qld, NSW, Vic, Tas.

SIZE: Male body length 4 mm, female 6 mm.

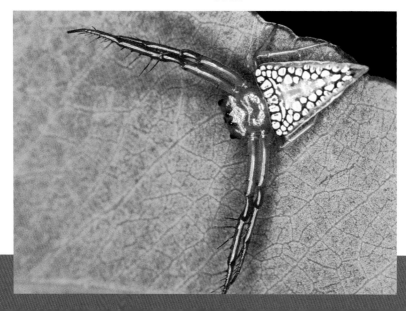

This species constructs ribbons of silk intersecting through the hub of the web in the shape of the cross of St Andrew. This structure, called a stabilimentum, is made of special silk which reflects ultraviolet light and is thought to play a role in attracting flying insects.

DESCRIPTION: The abdomen of the female (pictured) has broad bands of yellow, reddish-brown and white, with several rows of white spots. The cephalothorax is brownish with a dense covering of silvery hairs. The male is much smaller and less colourful than the female, without the yellow bands.

LIFE HISTORY: Mating takes place in the female's web and the male may lose one or more legs if the female is not receptive. One or two pear-shaped egg sacs are built by the female and hidden in foliage at the edge of the web.

Each greenish sac contains up to 300 eggs which hatch within three weeks. The young spiders disperse to construct their own webs, beginning with a spiral stabilimentum before constructing the more familiar cross shape.

BEHAVIOUR: This species sits in the centre of the web both day and night. If disturbed, the spider may shake the web so vigorously that it becomes a blur. It feeds on flying insects such as flies, bees and small beetles.

HABITAT: Found in heathlands, woodlands, dry forests and suburban areas.

VENOM: This species is not known to bite.

DISTRIBUTION: Qld, NSW, Vic, NT.

SIZE: Male body length 5 mm, female 12–15 mm.

Left: The underside of the female St Andrew's Cross Spider is as attractively patterned as the top side.

Bird-dropping Spider *Celaenia excavata*

This spider uses a remarkable method for capturing prey. It produces a scent which is identical to that produced by female Owlet Moths to attract males for mating. Consequently, the spider feeds almost exclusively on male moths which are lured unsuspectingly to their deaths.

DESCRIPTION: The male is tiny compared to the female, although they are similar in shape and colour. Both are mottled brown, cream and black, with a remarkable resemblance to bird droppings.

LIFE HISTORY: The female constructs up to ten round, brown and black egg sacs which she guards continuously. Despite this, the eggs are heavily parasitised by tiny wasps which leave minute holes as they exit the sac. This species does not build a web but sits in foliage producing a scent to attract males of the moth Family Noctuidae. The moths are grasped by the spider's heavily spined legs when within range. When mature, the male seeks out the female for mating.

BEHAVIOUR: Bird-dropping Spiders hide in foliage during the day and are active at night, but rarely leave their chosen position amongst foliage.

HABITAT: Found in dry forests, woodlands, orchards, agricultural and suburban areas. It is also known as the Orchard Spider, as it may be common in orchards feeding on pest moths.

VENOM: This species is not known to bite. It may cause a small local reaction.

DISTRIBUTION: Qld, NSW, Vic, Tas, SA.

SIZE: Male body length 2–3 mm, female 10–12 mm.

The Garden Orb-weaver is one of the largest and most common spiders in eastern Australia. It is familiar to most Australians who have walked through their webs, strung across paths, at night.

DESCRIPTION: This species is extremely variable in colour and pattern. Adults are generally grey-brown through light brown to orange-yellow, sometimes with white markings on the abdomen.

LIFE HISTORY: The female constructs a greenish egg sac, about 30 mm long, containing 200–300 eggs. The spiderlings disperse to construct tiny webs of their own and mature the following summer. The adult spider constructs a perfect orb-shaped web, usually 1–2 m off the ground between trees and often across pathways at night. The web is often eaten

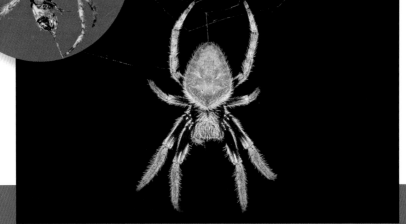

by the spider at dawn and a new web constructed the following night. Mating takes place in the female's web following courtship, and lasts up to 30 minutes.

BEHAVIOUR: Adults spin webs at dusk and remain in the hub of the web at night, moving only to ensnare prey or to retreat when disturbed. They feed on a wide range of flying insects caught in the web. During the day, they hide in foliage at the edge of the web.

HABITAT: Found in dry forest, woodland, heathland and suburban areas. This species can be extremely common.

VENOM: Bites are rare, causing only local temporary symptoms such as mild pain and swelling.

DISTRIBUTION: All States and Territories except Tasmania.

SIZE: Male body length 15–17 mm, female 20–25 mm.

Left: Male Garden Orb-weavers are smaller and sometimes appear hairier than the female.

Six-spined Spider
Austracantha minax

This species is also called a Spiny Spider, Jewel Spider or Christmas Spider, as it is most common around Christmas. Completely black (melanic) specimens, both male and female, sometimes occur.

DESCRIPTION: Males are darker and smaller than females with shorter and blunter spines. Males also have large, pear-shaped pedipalps.

LIFE HISTORY: The female constructs a reddish-brown egg sac about 25 mm long, containing 120–160 eggs, usually attached to a leaf or twig at the edge of her web. The tiny spiderlings are black and construct small communal webs, often in tall grass. They feed on small flying insects trapped in the web. The adult's web is no more than a metre above the ground and large aggregations of spiders may occur in low shrubs or grasslands, each web overlapping with the others. The web is often decorated with small balls of fluffy white silk, the purpose of which is unknown. Mating takes place within these communal webs.

BEHAVIOUR: Six-spined Spiders are active during the day but are usually confined to their webs. When disturbed, the spider will retreat to the edge of the web.

HABITAT: Found in dry forests, grasslands, woodlands and heathlands, particularly forests with a grassy understorey.

VENOM: These spiders are not aggressive and are known to bite only very rarely. The bite is mildly painful with only a local reaction.

DISTRIBUTION: All States and Territories.

SIZE: Male body length 3–4 mm, female 8–10 mm.

This spider was collected near Cooktown in Queensland, probably by Joseph Banks, on the Endeavour *voyage in 1770. It was the first spider to be collected and recorded by science from Australia.*

DESCRIPTION: Males are similar to females but are smaller and more black than yellow. The pattern and the brightness of the yellow is variable in both sexes and the size and shape of the spines is also variable.

LIFE HISTORY: The female produces a green, oval-shaped egg sac, 12–15 mm in diameter. Despite being the first species of spider described from Australia, very little is known about their biology, but it is probably very similar to the better-known Six-spined Spider. They appear to feed on small flying insects caught in their simple webs. There are often small balls of fluffy white silk throughout the web, the purpose of which is unknown. Mating probably takes place in the web of the female.

BEHAVIOUR: Black and Yellow Spiny Spiders remain in their webs and are active during the day. When disturbed, they retreat to the edges of the web.

HABITAT: Found in dry rainforests and woodlands. These spiders have an ability to disperse widely and survive in many areas of suitable habitat. Consequently they are also found in Papua New Guinea, Polynesia and other Pacific Islands.

VENOM: This species is not known to bite.

DISTRIBUTION: Queensland.

SIZE: Male body length 3–4 mm, female 8–10 mm.

Members of this genus are found in the tropical and subtropical areas of the world and they are well represented in Australia. Spiny Spiders are characterised by a very tough, shield-like covering to the abdomen which support six stout spines. They are also very colourful.

DESCRIPTION: This species is mostly black with a variable patch of white at the front of the abdomen. This white area is interspersed with black spots and lines of various shapes and sizes. The legs are short and are tucked underneath the cephalothorax when at rest or when threatened. Males are very small compared to the females (pictured) and are rarely seen.

LIFE HISTORY: As with many species of spiders from tropical Australia, very little is known of the biology and life history of this species. Like other spiny spiders (*Gasteracantha* spp.), mating probably takes place in the female's web and she constructs an egg sac attached to foliage close to the web. The egg sacs themselves have never been recorded.

BEHAVIOUR: The adult builds a small vertical orb web amongst low bushes and tall grass, particularly around marshes and swamps, where they catch small flying insects.

HABITAT: Found mainly in swampy areas.

VENOM: This species is not known to bite.

DISTRIBUTION: North Queensland.

SIZE: Male body length 1–3 mm, female 6–8 mm.

There are two species of camel spiders in Australia, so called because of the humped abdomen. They are beautifully coloured with silver, black and green on the abdomen, and pale green on the cephalothorax and legs.

DESCRIPTION: Males are similar to females (pictured) in colour, shape and pattern, but much smaller. There may be a pair of black tubercles (bumps) at the front of the abdomen. The colour of the cephalothorax may vary from yellowish to orange brown. Black bands may also occur on the legs.

LIFE HISTORY: Little is known about the biology and life history of these species. The female constructs a delicate horizontal orb web, 20–40 cm in diameter plus supporting threads, under which may be a smaller area of flimsy web. There may be a hole in the hub of the web in which the spider sits, upside down. The male's web is slightly smaller than that of the female. Mating probably takes place in the female's web.

BEHAVIOUR: The webs are made amongst low shrubs, usually close to creeks. They may also be constructed between reeds, a few centimetres above the water surface. They feed on small insects such as flies and moths caught in the web.

HABITAT: Found in dry and wet forests, woodlands and suburban areas.

VENOM: This species is not known to bite.

DISTRIBUTION: Qld, NSW, Vic.

SIZE: Male body length 4–6 mm, female 10–15 mm.

Golden Orb-weavers build the largest webs of any Australian spiders. Their webs often span several metres and are composed of rich golden silk which shines in the sunlight. The webs are strong enough to trap small birds and the spiders will sometimes feed on them, but they feed mainly on flying insects.

DESCRIPTION: The male is tiny compared to the female (pictured) and more brown than grey. Males are often visible within the female's web.

LIFE HISTORY: The female produces a fluffy golden egg sac in late summer or autumn, hidden in foliage at the edge of her web. The female dies soon after producing the sac and the spiderlings hatch and fend for themselves, constructing tiny orb webs to catch small flying insects. The web of the adult is enormous, with the catching area more than a metre across and the framework sometimes covering more than three metres. Several males may live on the opposite side of the web to the female, awaiting a chance to mate.

BEHAVIOUR: Golden Orb-weavers sit motionless in the centre of the web and retreat only to the edges when disturbed. They remain in this position both day and night.

HABITAT: Found in dry forest, woodland and suburban areas, particularly around streams and rivers.

VENOM: This species is unaggressive and bites are rare, causing only mild pain and nausea.

DISTRIBUTION: Qld, NSW, ACT, Vic, WA, NT.

SIZE: Male body length 4–6 mm, female 20–28 mm.

Leaf-curling Spider   *Phonognatha* spp.

Leaf-curling spiders construct a shelter in the centre of their webs to hide from birds and predatory insects. The shelter is usually made from a dead curled leaf, hoisted up from the ground, but empty snail shells, pieces of paper or plastic tape may also be used.

DESCRIPTION: The abdomen is smooth and light brown, sometimes with a white patch on top with darker brown markings. The cephalothorax and legs of the females are orange-brown but those of the males are a brighter red-brown.

LIFE HISTORY: The male seeks out the female and mating takes place inside or just outside her retreat. She then constructs an egg sac within another leaf and places it in foliage near the edge of her web. Unusually, she makes only one egg sac which contains up to 200 eggs. These hatch after 2–3 weeks and the spiderlings disperse after their first moult to construct their own webs.

BEHAVIOUR: This species remains in the retreat during the day and usually rebuilds the web each night. If severely disturbed, the spider will abandon the retreat and drop to the ground before scurrying off. They feed on moths, beetles, bees and flies caught in the web, both day and night.

HABITAT: Found in woodlands, heathlands and dry forests.

VENOM: Bites are rare but may cause localised pain and swelling.

DISTRIBUTION: Qld, NSW, Vic, Tas, SA.

SIZE: Male body length 5–6 mm, female 8–10 mm.

This species has a very unusual mating strategy. The female can only mate as soon as she has moulted into adulthood, as her exoskeleton quickly hardens to make mating impossible. Consequently one or more males must be standing by at the time of her final moult and the male who mates with her dies soon afterwards.

DESCRIPTION: The colour of this species varies considerably between individuals and also in different circumstances. The colour appears to change slightly when the spider is disturbed, pulsating on the outer edges. Males and females are similar in colour, but males are flatter and smaller.

LIFE HISTORY: The female constructs a long, brown egg sac, hidden in a loose tangle of silk near her web. It contains 45–70 cream-coloured eggs which hatch during summer. During the day the spider sits on the underside of a leaf with the legs held close to the body, well-camouflaged amongst foliage. At night the female sits in a small orb web, constructed between branches or amongst grass and shrubs close to the ground. The web is removed before dawn. Adult males do not build webs, but seek out immature females that are ready to moult into adulthood.

BEHAVIOUR: Females remain motionless during the day and are active, building small orb webs, at night. They feed on small, soft-bodied insects.

HABITAT: Found in dry forests, woodlands and heathlands.

VENOM: This species does not bite.

DISTRIBUTION: Qld, NSW, Vic.

SIZE: Male body length 2 mm, female 6–7 mm.

Wraparound Spiders   *Dolophones* spp.

Wraparound spiders are so called because their abdomen curves inwards underneath to allow the spider to wrap itself around a branch. With its flat body and legs held tightly together, the spider is almost impossible to see.

DESCRIPTION: There are at least twenty species of wraparound spiders in Australia, in a range of shapes and sizes. They are also called "leopard spiders", due to a number of shallow pits on the abdomen outlined by dark circles. Most species are light to dark brown or grey, their colour usually matching the colour of the branch on which they rest. The Turret Spider (*Dolophones turrigera*), also part of this group, has a small knob on top of its abdomen that resembles a broken-off twig.

LIFE HISTORY: Very little is known of the biology of most species within this group. The female constructs an egg sac containing about 50 eggs, made from woolly silk which is attached to a twig near her web. The spiderlings probably construct their own webs soon after dispersing.

BEHAVIOUR: Adults build a small orb web at night to catch small flying insects. The web is removed before dawn and the spider spends the day wrapped around a branch.

HABITAT: Found mainly in natural bushland such as dry forests and woodlands, rarely in suburban areas.

VENOM: These spiders are not known to bite.

DISTRIBUTION: All States and Territories.

SIZE: Male body length 5–8 mm, female 8–12 mm.

Top, left: Members of this group build a small orb web to catch flying insects, but these webs are rarely seen.

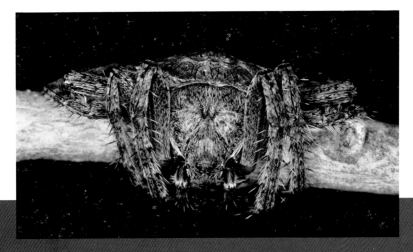

The Scorpion-tailed Spider has a greatly elongated abdomen which it curls over its body like a scorpion. When sitting in its web, it also resembles a small dried leaf or curl of bark.

DESCRIPTION: The abdomen of the female Scorpion-tailed Spider is long and cream coloured, ending with four small bumps at the tip. The abdomen also covers much of the small, brown cephalothorax. The abdomen of the male is not nearly as elongated as that of the female. Juveniles range in colour from pinkish to orange-yellow.

LIFE HISTORY: The web is built amongst low bushes and is rarely vertical like most orb-weavers, more often inclined at an angle or even horizontal. The female constructs a row of oval-shaped egg sacs in gaps in the upper half of the web, each sac containing about 60 eggs. The eggs hatch in early summer and the spiderlings begin to construct small webs nearby.

BEHAVIOUR: The female sits in the web during the day with legs held tightly to the body and the abdomen curled over slightly. It feeds on small insects caught in the web, such as flies and mosquitoes. Little is known of the male of this species.

HABITAT: Found in woodlands, dry forests and suburban areas.

VENOM: Bites are rare but may include local pain and swelling.

DISTRIBUTION: Qld, NSW, Vic, Tas, SA, WA.

SIZE: Male body length 3 mm, female 15 mm.

Long-jawed Spiders

Family: Tetragnathidae

Long-jawed Spiders   *Tetragnatha* spp.

Long-jawed spiders are long, cylindrical spiders with greatly enlarged chelicerae projecting in front of the head. Their pedipalps are also quite elongate. Most species are drab grey or brown, sometimes with tubercles or darker patterns on the abdomen.

HABITAT: Found in woodlands, wet forests and swamplands. They are largely restricted to eastern Australia.

BEHAVIOUR: Long-jawed spiders spend most of their time sitting immobile in their webs awaiting prey. They also sit with their bodies resting tightly against reed or grass stems. This affords them excellent camouflage.

WEB: Adults build horizontal or slightly angled orb webs amongst reeds or long grass, usually near water.

FEEDING HABITS: Long-jawed spiders feed on insects found near water, such as damselflies, adult caddisflies and moths.

BREEDING: Adults open up the chelicerae as they approach each other for mating and the legs meet stretched out to the sides of the body. The male keeps the female's chelicerae held open with special "teeth" on his chelicerae while he mates with her, ensuring she cannot consume him. Following mating, the female builds 2–3 small disc-shaped egg sacs attached to foliage.

NO. OF SPECIES: There are about twenty species of long-jawed spiders in Australia and more than 1000 species worldwide.

SIZE: Body length 7–15 mm.

Comb-footed Spiders
Family: Theridiidae

Red and Black Spider *Ambicodamus crinitus*

*This species is commonly mistaken for the Red-back Spider (*Latrodectus hasselti*) but there is no similarity other than being red and black. This species is smaller, a different shape and has a bright red cephalothorax.*

DESCRIPTION: Males and females are very similar in appearance but males are slightly smaller. The cephalothorax is red and the abdomen black with a bluish sheen.

LIFE HISTORY: The egg sac contains 30–50 cream-coloured eggs and has a woolly appearance. It is suspended in the web, which is just a few irregular strands of silk built under stones, logs or bark. The spider moves around on the underside of the web. This species does not make a web to catch prey, but wanders in and over bark, generally on tree trunks close to the ground,

searching for small insects. Males leave their shelters during summer and wander in search of females, sometimes accidentally entering houses where they may be confused with Red back Spiders.

BEHAVIOUR: Red and Black Spiders are active during the day. They move around searching for prey, stopping occasionally to rest.

HABITAT: Found in dry forest, particularly eucalypt forest. They are most commonly seen wandering on the bark of gum trees, particularly stringybarks.

VENOM: The bite is not dangerous, despite the red and black pattern which normally serves as a warning. It causes only a local reaction.

DISTRIBUTION: NSW, ACT, Vic, Tas.

SIZE: Male body length 10 mm, female 12 mm.

*This spider has been introduced from overseas and is widespread in suburban areas. Like the Grey House Spider (opposite), this species is often confused with the Red-back Spider (*Latrodectus hasselti*). It is also known as the Cupboard Spider.*

DESCRIPTION: The body varies from brown to black, usually with a dull white crescent-shaped mark on the top of the abdomen, along with a varying number of white or orange spots. Males are very similar to females, but much smaller and with more prominent white marks. While this species is often confused with the Red-back Spider, female Red-back Spiders always have a red mark on top of their abdomens and a distinctive red hourglass mark underneath.

LIFE HISTORY: The female produces a number of cream to yellow egg sacs, about 10 mm in diameter, attached to her web. The web, comprising a tangled network of strands attached to sticky threads in contact with the ground, is built inside cupboards or under furniture, or in sheds, amongst pot plants and in piles of rubbish. The sticky threads are used to trap passing prey such as crawling insects.

BEHAVIOUR: The spiders spend almost all the time in the web, becoming active at night and resting during the day.

HABITAT: Found mostly in suburban areas.

VENOM: The bite is not dangerous, but may temporarily cause headaches, nausea and small blisters around the bite.

DISTRIBUTION: All States and Territories.

SIZE: Male body length 4 mm, female 10 mm.

Grey House Spider *Achaearanea tepidariorum*

The Grey House Spider was introduced to Australia and is found throughout most of the world. There are a number of native species in the same genus (Achaearanea), but these are not found around houses and other dwellings, which is the domain of the Grey House Spider.

DESCRIPTION: The colour of the abdomen varies from creamy white to almost black, with six or more dark bands which also vary in colour. The cephalothorax and legs are yellow-brown with darker markings.

LIFE HISTORY: A tangled web is built in a protected site and small pieces of leaf may be incorporated into it. The male may stay in the female's web for some time before mating. Following mating, the female lays a number of pale brown, pear-shaped egg sacs up to 1 cm long. When the spiderlings hatch, they stay in the female's web (pictured) for a period before leaving to make small, regularly-shaped webs of their own.

BEHAVIOUR: Adults remain in the web both day and night, feeding on a range of small insects.

HABITAT: Found in suburban areas amongst rockeries, attached to fences but particularly under the eaves of houses. It is also very common to find this species in sheds and hiding in old furniture.

VENOM: This spider is not known to bite. However, as it is a similar shape to the Red-back Spider, it is often confused with this species.

DISTRIBUTION: All States and Territories.

SIZE: Male body length 7 mm, female 10 mm.

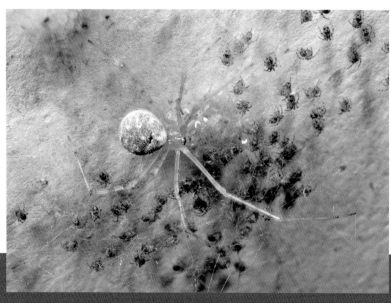

Red-back Spider   *Latrodectus hasselti*

The Red-back Spider is one of the best known spiders in Australia. It has made its way into songs, stories and verse and has become an important part of the Australian culture.

DESCRIPTION: The female is black and pea-shaped with long slender legs — she usually has a large red stripe on the back of her abdomen. There is also a red hourglass pattern underneath the abdomen. The male is tiny and very rarely seen.

LIFE HISTORY: During summer the female constructs 4–5 cream-coloured egg sacs, collectively containing up to 200 eggs. The spiderlings hatch after two weeks and disperse by ballooning. Females mature after 5–6 months and

Top: The red stripe on the back of the female's abdomen is sometimes very small and difficult to see.

may live three years, but males live only about six months. Prey includes any insects, spiders and even vertebrates such as lizards of suitable size. The web is generally built in corners and comprises a retreat funnel at the top, surrounded by messy strands of silk, leading to a number of thick sticky threads attached to the ground.

BEHAVIOUR: Red-back Spiders remain in the back of the retreat during the day and emerge towards the front at night.

HABITAT: Found in dry forest, woodland, agricultural and suburban areas.

VENOM: The Red-back Spider is one of Australia's most venomous spiders, causing at least thirteen deaths before an antivenom was developed. The bite causes sweating, muscle weakness and in severe cases vomiting, convulsions and coma.

DISTRIBUTION: All States and Territories.

SIZE: Male body length 2–3 mm, female 10–15 mm.

Glossary

ABDOMEN The last or final section of the body of an invertebrate.

ARACHNIDS A group of arthropods which includes spiders, scorpions, pseudoscorpions, mites, ticks, and harvestmen.

ARANEOMORPH A group of advanced spiders whose fangs move sideways in a horizontal axis. Most spiders fall into this group.

ARTHROPODS Joint-legged invertebrates with a body divided into segments, such as arachnids, insects and crustaceans.

BALLOONING A process where spiderlings send out a line of silk to be carried away by the wind, enabling the spiderling to travel long distances.

BOOK LUNGS Breathing structures located under the abdomen of spiders. Oxygen is absorbed by layers of gill-like plates arranged like the pages of a closed book.

CEPHALOTHORAX A fusion of the head and thorax of spiders.

CHELICERAE The first pair of appendages in spiders; short thick structures that hold the fangs.

CRIBELLUM A seive-like plate covering the spinnerets of "cribellate" spiders.

EXOSKELETON The tough outer covering of spiders, literally an external skeleton.

FAMILY A group of closely related genera.

FOLIAGE The leaves and branches of trees and shrubs.

GENUS (PLURAL GENERA) A group of closely-related species.

HUB The area of a web, usually at or near the centre, where the spokes of the web meet.

INVERTEBRATE An animal without a backbone.

MIMICRY A process by which one species resembles another species (by looks, scent, behaviour).

MOULT To shed skin and replace with new skin.

MYGALOMORPH A group of primitive, mostly ground-dwelling spiders, whose fangs move up and down like daggers.

NOCTURNAL Active at night.

ORDER A group of closely-related families of animals.

PARASITE An animal completely dependent on the body of another animal for its food, usually feeding without killing its host.

PARASITOID A parasite that develops within the body of its host, eventually killing it.

PEDIPALPS Small segmented appendages at the front of the cephalothorax used during mating and as touch, scent and taste receptors.

PHEROMONES A chemical smell given off by an animal, usually by females to attract males for mating.

SCLEROTIN A dark compound which strengthens the outer layer of the spider exoskeleton.

SPECIES A group that shares the same physical features and can interbreed to produce fertile young.

SPIGOTS Tiny, valve-like glands which make up the spinnerets of spiders. Each spigot is attached to a silk glad and controls the production of silk.

SPINNERETS Segmented, finger-like appendages at the tip of a spider's abdomen, from which silk is extruded.

SPIRACLES Small openings in the body of a spider used for breathing.

STABILIMENTUM Broad ribbons of thick silk, usually in the shape of a cross or circle, spun in the centre of a spider's web.

TUBERCLE A small bump on the outer layers of a spider's exoskeleton.

VERTEBRATES Animals with backbones.

Index

Links & Further Reading

Books

Child, J. *Australian Spiders (third edition),* Periwinkle Books, Sydney, 1977

Clyne, D. *A Guide to Australian Spiders,* Thomas Nelson Ltd, Melbourne, 1969

Davies, V.T. *Australian Spiders: Collection, Preservation and Identification,* Queensland Museum, Brisbane, 1986

Hawkeswood, T.J. 2003, *Spiders of Australia: an Introduction to their Classification, Biology and Distribution,* Pensoft Publishing, Bulgaria, 2003

Koch, L.E. *The Red-Back Spider and Other Venomous Creatures,* Western Australian Museum, Perth, 1980

Lindsey, T. *Spiders of Australia,* New Holland Publishers Pty Ltd, Sydney, 1998

Main, B.Y. *Spiders of Australia,* Jacaranda Press, Brisbane, 1964

Main, B.Y. *Spiders (second edition),* William Collins Pty Ltd, Sydney, 1984

Mascord, R. *Australian Spiders in Colour,* Reed Books, Sydney, 1970

McKeown, K.C. *Spider Wonders of Australia,* Angus & Robertson Ltd, Sydney (out of print), 1936

Simon-Brunet, B. *The Silken Web: A Natural History of Australian Spiders,* Reed Books, Sydney, 1994

Staunton, I. *All About Australian Spiders,* Ure Smith Pty Ltd, Sydney, 1968

Walker, K.L. Yen, A.L. & Milledge, G.A. *Spiders and Scorpions Commonly Found in Victoria,* Royal Society of Victoria, Melbourne, 2003

Websites

Australian Museum Spider fact sheets
www.amonline.net.au/factsheets/index.htm#spiders

Spiders of South-East Queensland
www.qm.qld.gov.au/features/spiders/index.asp

The Find-a-Spider Guide
www.usq.edu.au/spider/index.htm

Victorian Spiders
museumvictoria.com.au/spiders/

Australasian Arachnological Society
www.australasian-arachnology.org/

The Wolf Spiders of Australia
www.lycosidae.info/identification/australia/firstpage.html

Spider bites
www.usyd.edu.au/anaes/venom/spiders.html

Australian Venom Research Unit
www.avru.org/

Acknowledgements

I am deeply grateful to Julie, Georgia, Michael and Holly Honan for their continued support. Many thanks to Melbourne Zoo and the Keith Turnbull Research Institute for access to some of the specimens photographed.

— Patrick Honan

Published by Steve Parish Publishing Pty Ltd
PO Box 1058, Archerfield, Queensland 4108
Australia

www.steveparish.com.au

© Steve Parish Publishing

ISBN: 978174193408 3

First printed in 2008

Principal Photographer: Patrick Honan

Front cover image: Green Tree Ant-mimicking
Spider
Title page main image: Wolf Spider. Inset, top to
bottom: Red-back Spider; Jumping Spider

Text: Patrick Honan
Editing: Kerry McDuling; Michele Perry,
Helen Anderson, SPP
Design: Thomas Hamlyn-Harris, SPP
Production: Tina Brewster, SPP

Prepress by Colour Chiefs Digital Imaging,
Brisbane, Australia
Printed in Singapore by Imago

**Produced in Australia at the Steve Parish
Publishing Studios**